SO-DTA-288

Developing and Writing

your

Thesis, Dissertation or Project

A book of sound advice about conceptualizing,
organizing, developing and finalizing your
terminal graduate research

William G. Webster, Sr.

For Master's and Doctoral candidates who need help crossing that last threshold...

Copyright © 1998 by William Gerald Webster, Sr.

Library of Congress Catalog Card Number: 98-92756

ISBN: 0-9663667-0-0

All rights reserved. No part of this book may be reproduced or transmitted in any form or by any means, electronic or mechanical, including photocopying, recording, or by any information storage or retrieval system, without written permission from Academic Scholarwrite Consulting and Publishing, except for inclusion of quotations in a review.

Printed in the United States of America

HOW TO ORDER
Single copies may be ordered from Academic Scholarwrite Publishing, P.O. Box 1844, San Ramon, CA 94583. Quantity discounts are available for some purchasers. Your letterhead should include information concerning the intended use of the books as well as the number of books you wish to purchase.

Contents

Dedication

I dedicate this book to NILS GUSTAVE HAGBERG I, (1916 --) and MARGARET ELIZABETH HAGBERG (1916-1996) whose wisdom and support at a crucial juncture in my life helped me to "turn an important corner" in both my professional and personal development. Every person has one or more noteworthy "significant others;" and Nils and "Marge" helped me on more than one occasion.

Nils immigrated to America, to Chicago, from Sweden with his family at the age of seven. He and Marge married in 1937. Armed with the love and support of Marge, coupled with faith in the future of America, Nils overcame several major obstacles to become the founder of one of the most successful metal stamping and manufacturing firms in the nation.

I am thankful for their friendship. I am also proud to include the names of these two fine persons in the permanent record of the Library of Congress.

About the Author

Dr. WILLIAM G. WEBSTER, Sr. started writing professionally because of jobs that required writing. While Assistant Superintendent of Schools in the Oakland (California) Unified School District, he wrote editorials as well as articles for a bi-monthly school district newspaper called *Urban Education.* He found that the kind of writing required for the paper was extremely different from that required for his Master's thesis at California State University, Hayward, which he earned many years earlier.

While still in that position---in 1972---he published a novel, *One by One,* with Doubleday. Although he did not follow that up with another novel, he knew that writing was the way to go. It was in his blood!

After completing his dissertation and Doctorate at the University of the Pacific, he joined the faculty of California State University, Stanislaus. For almost 23 years, he taught *Research Methods* and *Thesis,* two related courses designed to help students with their theses, projects and dissertations.

During the years at Stanislaus State (the local popular name of the University), he founded the *School of Education Journal,* then a quarterly, but now a refereed annual theme-driven scholarly journal. During his 19-year tenure as Editor of the Journal, he wrote more than 25 articles related to its content. He also wrote two graduate-level textbooks: *Effective Collective Bargaining in Public Education* (Iowa State University Press, 1985) and *Learner-Centered Principalship: The Principal as Teacher of Teachers* (Praeger Publishers, 1994).

These experiences led to the publication of this book and its companion volume, *21 Models for Developing and Writing Dissertations, Theses and Projects.* These two volumes contain virtually all that he has learned about helping students with conceptualizing, organizing, developing, and finalizing their graduate research and writing requirements.

Acknowledgement

I have not attempted to cite in the text all of the authorities and sources consulted in the preparation of this book. In addition to the interrupted narrative flow, doing so would require much more space than is available. The list would include many authors, periodicals, industrial organizations, libraries, and many departments of the federal government.

Many people contributed to the development of this book. The people at the library at Stanislaus State have been invaluable. They have helped with their willingness (no, *eagerness*) to unearth documents and generally, to help me with the mechanics of research---not to mention the various wrinkles related to remote library access with the computer. For this support, I thank Laura Boyer, Rick Dietz, Bob Santos, Art Buell, and Paula Crawford.

On many occasions, I exchanged ideas with some of my colleagues. This list includes Drs. John Borba, Diana Demetrulias, Granger Dinwiddie, Tod Anton, Dawn Poole, Mimi Bradley, Juan Flores, Doni Kobus, Kathleen Galbo, Joan Wink, Janet Towell, Connie Kane, Elmano Costa, Larry Giventer, Rich Luevano, Fay Shin, Pam Russ, Brenda Betts, Sharon Brockman, Leo Hernandez and Tony Vang.

Many of my students over the years have brought many real-world research ideas from their daily experiences of running schools. This list of present and former students includes David Yeakle, Kathy Berkeley, Mike Chimente, Ann Cecchetti, Tony Borba, Teresa Roberson, Doug Dorman, Meg Bozarth, Judith Cochran, Steve Betando, Iris Haapanen, Mai Xiong, Linda Youngmayr, Dennis Jones, Gail Mazzucchelli, Rodney Owen, Terina Harrison, Ingrid Hjelmervik, Dru Howenstine, Diane Hernandez-Dutra, Dee Johnson, Irma Lawrence, Rich Fonseca, Karen Smith, Jay Hays, Patrick Anastasio, Rosemarie Melo, Mary McCandless, Alice Campbell, Lucille Porter, Ann Slattery, Suzan Turner, Maureen Vieth, Maryse Padovani, Don Halseth, Rosemary Parga, Annarae Luevano, Barney Hale, Nan Beattie, Debra Marvulli, Melody Ho, Janis Morehead and Cheri Conaway. I sincerely thank these and all of my former students. Because they let me help them, I developed many if not most of the ideas for this book.

Warning---Disclaimer

This book was written to provide information related to the subject matter covered. It is sold with the understanding that the author and publisher are not engaged in rendering legal, accounting or other related professional services.

It is not the purpose of this book to reprint all information that is otherwise available to you as a graduate student. Rather, this book is intended to complement, amplify and supplement other texts. Throughout this book, you will see in boldface many excellent references related to topics under discussion. You are urged to read them and all available material. You are urged to learn as much as possible about developing your required graduate document and to tailor information to your individual needs. More information is offered in the Appendix.

The matter of developing and writing your dissertation, thesis or project has no shortcuts, no formulas or easy-out schemes. Anyone who must write an approved scholarly study must expect to invest a lot of time and effort. This book and its companion volume are aids, important resources, but they are not substitutes for intelligent, diligent application of time and effort.

Every effort has been made to make this book usable, easy-to-understand and as accurate as possible. However, there may be mistakes both typographical and in content. Therefore, this book should be used as a general guide and not as the ultimate source of information related to development and writing your dissertation, thesis or project. Furthermore, the information in this book is timely only up to its printing date.

The purpose of this book is to educate. The author and Academic Scholarwrite publishing shall have neither liability nor responsibility to any person or entity with respect to any loss or damage caused, or alleged to be caused, directly or indirectly by the information contained in this book.

OTHER BOOKS BY WILLIAM G. WEBSTER

21 Models for Developing and Writing Theses, Dissertations and Projects. (Academic Scholarwrite, 1998)

Learner-Centered Principalship: The Principal as Teacher of Teachers. (Praeger Publishers, 1994)

Effective Collective Bargaining in Public Education: (Iowa State University Press, 1985)

One by One (A novel, Doubleday and Co., 1972)

1

Introduction and Mindset

You have acquired this book, an indication that you might be running into problems finishing your thesis, dissertation or project. It is also likely that you have run the gauntlet of coursework with at least a "B" average, and that you fit one of two categories. You could be a student who finished your Bachelor's degree and went directly to work on your master's or doctorate. Just as likely, you might be a re-entry student, a person with considerable experience in the work world who needs a Master's degree or, less likely, a doctoral degree for job advancement.

In either case, this book is appropriate for you. Theses and dissertations are standard requirements in quality colleges and universities. This book, together with its companion volume, *21 Models for Developing and Writing Theses, Dissertations and Projects,* offers many ideas and solutions for accomplishing terminal scholarly graduate writing requirements.

It is an unfortunate fact that the majority of institutions of higher education fail to give adequate support and guidance to graduate students during development of their theses, dissertations or projects. Why? The answer to that question requires complicated responses that involve the culture of the professorship, the early education of students, and several other factors. This book explores these questions, but only to the extent necessary to help students avoid certain pitfalls and dangers as they learn to move methodically and rapidly toward completion of their theses, dissertations or projects. After all, that is your central interest is receiving the degree and returning to the world of work. Right?

The limits of this book: A few disclaimers

Nothing in this book or its title means that you should compromise or somehow weaken the quality of your thesis, dissertation or project. Early completion of terminal scholarly activities, one of the advantages discussed in this book, does not mean or require a compromise of quality.

No book can *guarantee* success in completion of theses or dissertations, and this one is no exception. Rather, it will help you by offering insights into pitfalls to avoid, together with alternative routes to successful completion. However, it is always important to remember that success is the result of diligent application of your time, talent and energy in a systematic way.

The fictitious titles used throughout this book are from my imagination and experiential background. There is always the possibility that one or more of these titles will appear to be similar to one or more existent theses or dissertations. Because of this possibility, it is important to make the explicit statement here that any similarities to existent theses are purely coincidental.

These fictitious titles are teaching devices, created to enhance the conceptual grasp of readers. Because of this, readers who are very knowledgeable about the literature of their fields might perceive one or more of these titles as simple or even simplistic. Thus, I extend an apology beforehand.

It is important to make a point about certain grammatical usages in this book. Language purists challenge use of the passive voice with arguments that it is "backwards," awkward and uses more words. Still, the passive voice persists in scholarly writing in most fields. Check your textbooks and other scholarly vehicles for confirmation of this. Thus, while the text of this book avoids the passive voice, many of the extracts, facsimiles, and examples of theses and dissertations use it quite freely.

There was no attempt to have the extracts, facsimiles and examples of terminal studies conform to the dictates of this or that style manual. This was quite deliberate, intended to make the point that many formats are possible.

Equally deliberate was the omission of many direct source citations in this book. Unlike many books in this broad area, I made no attempt to pay allegiance to this or that great scholar or tradition. A resulting benefit was better narrative flow, without the disruption of citations. You will find an ample number of sources in the Bibliography.

Finally, this is not a book about writing or form and style, although it contains many exemplars of good formal writing that students can use. Although your department is likely to require a specific manual of form and style, an excellent "starter" book on form and style is

Slade, C. 1997. *Form and Style:Research Papers, Reports, Theses.* Boston: Houghton-Mifflin.

Keeping statistics in proper perspective. A few words are appropriate here about statistics in connection with this book and its companion volume, *21 Models for Developing and Writing Theses, Dissertations and Projects.* For many reasons discussed throughout this book, graduate students tend toward overuse of statistics in particular and quantification in general.

There seems little doubt that the professiorate leans toward research that is number-heavy. In depth discussion of the reasons for this are numerous; indeed, they could fill volumes.

Words here are for the student consumers of this book. There is a strong possibility that you, too, will be under considerable pressure to include quantification in your study. If so, you must be realistic; after all, you need the support of those who advise and mentor you during development of your thesis, dissertation or project.

My interest here is encouragement of a certain mindset as you read this book and its companion volume. That mindset? Strive for *conceptual grasp* of the important elements that go into terminal scholarly graduate documents.

Conceptual grasp of the content of these books is critically important for three reasons. First, it will keep your "mental doorway" open for two compatible possibilities, *qualitative* research and *non-experimental* research. Second and equally important, you will avoid the dangerous tendency of limiting and "forcing" your ideas into "fitting" one or more of several statistics. After all, statistics are means, not ends. Third, there is a strong possibility that you can combine both qualitative and quantitative approaches in your final document.

Each college and university is unique. This book cannot be consistent with the specific guidelines for proposals and theses established by any one college or university. Why? Because there are almost as many formats, styles, criterion levels and other requirements associated with theses and dissertations as there are colleges and universities throughout the world.

A considerable portion of this book emphasizes student awareness of the dynamics of higher education bureaucracies. It is safe to say that those bureaucracies are more alike than different. However, organizational arrangements vary from school to school. Some schools accept proposed studies on the basis of informal discussion without documentation, while others require written scholarly proposals. Similarly, institutions vary in the amount of ongoing help and support offered. So, take the content of this book with a "grain of salt," and modify that content to fit the situation in which you find yourself.

The strengths of this book

This book is a practical manual for persons in various stages of development of Master's theses, dissertations or projects as required by the colleges and universities they attend. For that reason, it is simple and to-the-point, avoiding the excess baggage of scholarly pretentiousness.

For those of you who already have topics and research designs approved by committees of professors, the book can serve as a resource that will provide solutions to problems and routes around barriers encountered. Its greatest strength is simplicity in several important areas. These areas range from suggestions for developing topics to improvement in scholarly writing style.

This book will be most effective when used in conjunction with its companion volume, *21 Models for Developing and Writing Theses, Dissertations and Projects.* That practical book, loaded with ideas about ways to approach your terminal study, is available through the same avenues as this one.

Throughout the process, this manual will serve as a resource to which to return at different stages. The examples offered throughout will almost certainly point to a solution to a problem.

Quality colleges and universities regard theses and dissertations as significant contributions to knowledge within a field, indicators of student ability to conduct and present accurate research in a scientific, scholarly manner.

Let's face it: universities and colleges differ markedly as to the importance of thesis, dissertation or project requirements. The extremes range from high-quality, rigorous requirements to no terminal scholarly requirements at all. However, it is pretty safe to say that virtually all of the institutions that enjoy strong reputations require some kind of terminal scholarly activities. Most require theses and dissertations at the Master's and doctoral levels, respectively.

Theses and dissertations are original investigations within fields of interest. Although students write theses and dissertations under the close supervision of one or more advisers, one primary expectation is that they are products of student work performed independently.

From the standpoint of universities and colleges awarding degrees, theses and dissertations have additional purposes, well beyond the singular requirement of original research. Most graduate institutions recognize and encourage several other hoped-for outcomes of advanced study on theses and dissertations. Among these are:

1. Improvement in your ability to interpret and synthesize information.

2. Enhancement of your knowledge and presentation skills related to research methods.

3. Improvement of your knowledge of the ethics of research, especially with respect to the ownership of intellectual property.

Requirements as to form and style, length, and documentation standards vary from department to department, from discipline to discipline, and from institution to institution. Length requirements vary also. While some colleges and universities try to restrict the length of theses and dissertations to 150 and 300 pages respectively, others have no such restrictions. One dissertation at Stanford (Hagberg 1982) was 774 pages long!

Variations found in form and style usually are those peculiar to various disciplines. Those of you who have written a number of term papers within a discipline will easily learn its form, style and documentation requirements.

Prestige accrediting agencies view the quality of theses and dissertations produced at an institution as extremely important evidence of the quality of that institution.

Despite these variations, all colleges and universities that require theses, dissertations or projects view them as major components of the rites of passage into peer acceptance. Once you complete yours, you will feel the deep satisfaction of that recognition and acceptance.

What are realistic goals for your terminal scholarly studies? You must select a topic that is (1) an original, meaningful contribution to the field; (2) acceptable to a committee of faculty members; and (3) feasible within a reasonable time span. These requirements are amplified later in this chapter.

A terminal scholarly activity is a big order for most students, because of the criteria involved. Yes, it is likely that this task will seem formidable to you, but it is feasible if you have met minimal requirements in graduate coursework. This is my belief, based on many actual experiences with students. Many were persons of average of even below average ability!

***Generalizability* is the central interest of *all* theses and dissertations. Without it, scholarly efforts amount to little more than factual findings, with greatly reduced potential for impact that improves practice.**

Consistent with the major goals of science, theses and dissertations must serve the dual ends of *explanation* and *prediction* related to the phenomena studied. Researching scientists focus on the probability that antibiotics will be just as effective *all* similar hospital contexts, not just one. Similarly, classroom researchers who find that a certain basal reader is particularly effective in one school want to know whether that reader will be effective in other similar schools. In each example, researchers seek to predict or *generalize* as to the applicability of their findings in other situations. Eisner and Peshkin (1990, 171) characterized generalizations as ideas or images that enable prediction.

Generalizability means the extent to which research findings are applicable to reasonably similar situations. It is sometimes called *transferability* by some qualitative researchers (See Lincoln and Guba 1985).

It is safe to say that the quest for generalizability constitutes much of the basic stimulus for predictive effort in research. Without generalizability, scholarly activity is fact-gathering, with outcomes that amount to no more than free-standing factual curios that are not relevant for prediction purposes.

Many persons overlook the generalizability requirement. Faculty thesis committee members sometimes approve studies that are not theses. For example, one student received permission from her thesis committee and started a study called, *The History of the Education Department of _____ College, 1955-1990.* During a faculty meeting announcing and describing upcoming theses, another professor challenged this topic, arguing that it did not constitute a thesis. His major point was that it was no more than a detailed historical report. This professor argued, correctly, that it deserved the status of a project, not thesis, because it lacked generalizability. The majority of the members of the department upheld his position.

Generalizability in some theses and dissertations is not always as clearly evident as in that example. Consider the title, *An Analysis of the Relationship Between Exercise Fads and the Economic History of the United States, 1900-1990.* Where is the hoped-for generalizability of such a study?

The generalizability is in the patterns of connection between the history of exercise fads and the economic history of the United States. When and if researchers find several patterns of definite *co-occurrences*, the research has one or several generalizations about historical co-occurrences to offer to other historians interested in one or both of the topics. In turn, these historians might cautiously cite these co-occurrences as reasonably reliable patterns applicable to other historical events.

In order to conceptualize the intended generalizability of your study, think of other situations similar to your study context, and how the findings of your study might help them.

Theses and dissertations are models. You will satisfy the generalizability requirement if you think of your thesis or dissertation as a *model.*. This means that the generalizations you intend to derive from your research could serve as predictors, exemplars, patterns, frameworks, procedural models, prototype development and ideals that can guide practice in the field you studied.

Let's look at a few examples using fictitious thesis topics. One is a thesis topic in public administration, entitled *Education Levels of Large City Managers as Major Determinants of Their Attitudes Toward Public Employee Bargaining.* The generalizations derived from such a study might give added insights to city councils when hiring city managers, perhaps in the direction of added or higher education requirements of applicants. Similarly, businesses faced with the problem of retraining certain skilled workers might find quite useful the generalizations developed in a thesis entitled *Retraining Adaptability of Tool-and-Die Specialists as a Function of Years of Experience in the Trade* . The same is true of state legislatures that might change their minimum age kindergarten entry requirements after reviewing the generalizations revealed in a thesis entitled *The*

Relationship Between Ages at Kindergarten Entry and Behavior of Elementary School Boys.

The important point above is that all three of these theses offered *generalizability,* general findings that might serve as models or portions of models for future behaviors of the concerned agencies, or any others who perceive their situations as similar. Again, I encourage you to think of the long term, of *where the results of your study could possibly be applied,* for that constitutes a major portion of the basis of the value of all theses and dissertations.

While there are no formulas for determining generalizability or replicability of research outcomes, there are research design aspects that can enhance their likelihood. We will revisit the notion of generalizability in the applied sense throughout this book.

You must understand the distinctions between as well as the scope of theses, dissertations and projects.

Students who understand the distinctions between theses, dissertations and projects enjoy clear advantages when attempting to "dream creatively." The main advantage is clear conceptualization of their ideas because they understand clearly the expectations for each type of venture.

Let's clarify the similarities and differences. A *thesis* is a proposition based on a specific view of an aspect of a field, embodying the results of original research, advanced and defended by cogent argument. A *dissertation* is an *extended* thesis, far more comprehensive in scope, argument and intended generalizability. However, the extent of comprehensiveness of both theses and dissertations varies, dependent on the philosophical and professional outlooks of faculty advisors. In turn, these outlooks of faculty members are reflections of the quality of the college or university.

Theses and projects differentiated. Colleges and universities vary considerably with respect to their terminal scholarly requirements at the Master's level. Some require theses, while others permit either theses or projects. Let's use a brief sidebar here for distinguishing between the two scholarly ventures.

The major difference between a project and thesis is *extent of generalizability.* Projects usually apply to specific areas, communities, school districts, hospitals and other organizations with similar demographic conditions. Typically, projects are manuals, guidelines, directories, curricular frameworks and other outcomes immediately useful and applicable to certain agencies.

On the other hand, theses usually focus on broadly *generalizable* findings usable in most if not all similar organizations engaged in a given activity. Theses result in generalized findings related to how to solve problems confronted by many similar agencies or how to produce certain products needed by those agencies. On the other hand, projects result in actual *products*.

This means that the findings resulting from theses are more likely to have widespread applicability. For example, in a public water district a project might be *A Three-Month Procedure for Maximizing Watershed Containment in An Upper San Joaquin Valley Reservoir,* while a corresponding thesis might be *An Experience-Based Model for Maximizing Water Containment in Reservoirs in Two West Coast States.* Similarly, in a school district a project might be *A Procedural Manual for Hiring, Training and Assigning Bilingual Spanish Instructional Aides in San Joaquin County Schools,* while a corresponding thesis might be *A Model for Effective Employment of Bilingual Spanish Aides.*

Projects are context-specific, while the generalizability inherent in theses affords widespread applicability. In the examples above, both projects are demographically specific and thus geographically limited, while both theses offer the important advantage of generalizability or widespread applicability to many other contexts. This means that the project (above) related to Bilingual Spanish aides would have to be based on the policies, procedures, salaries and other considerations in a specific school district. By contrast, the thesis related to Bilingual Spanish aides could be usable in several states where Bilingual Spanish aides are commonplace.

A realistic look at the scope of theses, dissertations and projects. Most students start off with exceedingly ambitious topics that are too broad in scope. This costly error is due to two things. One is a general misconception about the realistic intentions of both theses and dissertations, and the second is lack of clarity about the differences between these terminal scholarly activities. Together, these misunderstandings interfere with or muddle creativity, called "dreaming creatively" throughout this book.

You should understand that these terminal scholarly activities *do not totally revolutionize thinking* in their fields. Rather, they expand the knowledge base of a field through countless small additions to that knowledge base.

It is neither possible nor desirable to write about *every* aspect of a problem or area of study. Still, over-ambitiousness is the most common problem found in the early drafts of thesis or dissertation proposals. It might be a problem for you as well.

> *Even if you fail to support the hypotheses of your study, you still have a thesis or dissertation. Why? Because it is still important to inform the literature of your field about the non-supported hypotheses!*

Over-ambitiousness in topic coverage often leads to several more problems, many of which may not show up until you are deep into your study. Those problems are:

1. Dilution, to the extent that findings are not definitive.

2. Generalizations are difficult if not impossible.

3. Students experience feelings of being overwhelmed. Usually, the research they have chosen is too multifaceted.

It is possible to illustrate the dangers of over-ambitiousness with a (fictitious) proposed topic, *A Validated Curriculum Alignment Procedure for Elementary Curricula*. The central interest of the study is development of a curriculum alignment procedure (for teacher use) in a school. After applying the procedure, the achievement performance in that school will be compared with achievement performance in another demographically comparable school with no systematically aligned curriculum. An interesting study? Yes. Achievable as a Master's thesis or even a doctoral dissertation? No!

The very scope of the study is the reason for the negative. Such a study would not be achievable with the ordinary resources available to graduate students. Taking such a proposed topic to completion would involve all elementary subjects, all elementary grade levels in a school, extended inservice sessions for aligning all curricula, and a comprehensive testing program for purposes of validating the curriculum alignment procedure. The logistics of such a study would be mind-boggling, especially in light of the resources and controls ordinarily available to M.A. students. The task in the example above would even be far more than should be expected of a doctoral dissertation!

Now let's put "boundaries" around the same study. Suppose we altered the proposed topic, to: *A Validated Curriculum Alignment Procedure for 5th Grade Mathematics Curricula*. This revised topic would be much more feasible for a Master's thesis. Expectations for a dissertation along the same lines would logically be more comprehensive than those for a Master's, and might extend to inclusion of all elementary grades. *A Validated Curriculum Alignment Procedure for Mathematics Curricula, 1-6* might be a good example of the scope of a doctoral dissertation written in the same sphere of interest. Carrying the example further, a typical Master's degree *project* related to the same content area might be, *A 5th Grade Mathematics Curriculum Guide and Activity Handbook for Marshall School.*

Students run into similar problems in other fields of study. Consider the challenge faced by a Business student interested in a thesis that seeks to identify experiences common to successful female top-level managers or executives in the interest of developing generalizations about those experiences. While one interesting topic might be, *Breaking Through the Glass Ceiling: Patterns of Vertical Mobility of Top-Level Female Managers*, the topic is too broad, for two reasons:

1. The requirements of vertical mobility in extremely different businesses might fail to yield patterns that offer the promise of generalizability.

2. The "glass ceiling" included in the title might be lower or higher, depending on the specifics of the business---- again, defying patterns which lead to cautious, useful generalizations.

Now suppose we change the topic to, *Breaking Through the Glass Ceiling: Patterns of Vertical Mobility of 100 Top-Level Female Bank Managers.* Immediately, the two problems addressed in (1) and (2) above disappear because of the delimited scope of the study. A study like this would appear to be appropriate in scope and comprehensiveness for a good Master's thesis. Similarly, an example of a dissertation in the same sphere of interest could be *Characteristic Career Paths of Top-Level Female Financial Officers of "Fortune 500" Companies.*

As will be clarified in the next section, the obvious difference between theses and dissertations, brought out by this example, is breadth. While the thesis focused only on female bank managers, the dissertation expanded to financial officers, a category that includes many bank managers as well as other specific high-level fiscal managers. However, the most powerful difference is in the potential for far more generalizations that could include most of the financial field.

The line between requirements for theses and dissertations is not well-defined. Frequently, the distinction between a thesis and a dissertation is a judgment, made by your Study Committee.

One more point needs emphasis here. Institutions vary considerably; thus, scope and content that suffice as a dissertation in one institution might not in another.

Before starting, you must understand the challenges of completing theses, dissertations or projects.

Your understanding of the exact barriers and problems you will face during your terminal scholarly studies will enhance your chances of quick completion. You have already completed a great deal of effort in coursework, but it is the energy you expend in doing your terminal research that will make your earlier effort pay.

Unfortunately, many good students are unclear about how to direct their energies when embarking on the matter of writing theses, dissertations or projects. When you understand the challenges, you can devise ways of overcoming them. The major ones are described here.

First, you must *select and develop an original topic that results in a contribution to the field.* Your research effort must add to what is known about the topic you choose. More often than not, relatively small contributions are the rule rather than the exception. The central idea, however, is that countless small additions to the knowledge base of a field lead to steady evolution in thinking in the field.

The unfortunately reality is that many students have trouble being creative because they have been *trained* to *not* think creatively. Most teaching methods reward low-level responses that "parrot" the teacher, in dull true-false, completion, matching and multiple choice tests----or in classroom responses. In most cases, precise words were emphasized and even rewarded. While it is true that some content must be taught at those low levels, it is unfortunate that many students are never given opportunities to be creative and original in their classroom responses and activities.   These same persons run into problems with *divergent* or creative production (See Orlich et. al. 1985, 169 or Guilford 1967, 5, 171-72; 214-16).).

Next, you must *develop a feasible topic and related research approach.* A feasible topic is one that can be completed within the context of time and resources available. If you are like most graduate students, you have a limited time span for completion of your studies.

One of the major mistakes made by many students is failure to anticipate the major problems incidental to carrying out investigations required by their thesis or doctoral interests.   Typically, students frequently fail to anticipate (1) attrition of and changes in study samples; (2) lack of identifiable population groups; (3) inability to gain direct access to respondents; and most importantly, (4) the time required to conduct certain studies. The only solution is careful assessment of likely obstacles *before* research is underway.   Often, chairpersons and committee members are helpful along these lines; however, as I have said repeatedly, institutions vary and committee members vary.   Students would do well to become self-reliant and attempt to anticipate these and other problems before getting too deep into their research.

You must also *develop a literary "style" commensurate with the traditions of high-quality terminal scholarly productivity.* Matters of literary style and adherence to scholarly standards are thoroughly addressed in several chapters in this book.   For this reason, they will not be discussed here.

Fourth, you must *select and work effectively with a thesis, dissertation or project committee* that serves a positive role of informed oversight and advocacy of your research interest. This is an extremely important topic that usually is overlooked in the literature related to development of scholarly terminal activities. Working with your committee is discussed at length in Chapter 5.

Finally, *you must complete the study within the context of college or university standards* for theses, dissertations and projects in matters of documentation, formatting and other style aspects. While this should not be difficult, awareness of its importance will help you to avoid problems.

Don't let all of this discourage you. The solutions to these problems are found throughout the book.

Students who successfully complete theses, dissertations or projects are those who aggressively "take charge" of their own progress while maintaining and projecting attitudes of optimism and confidence.

Many doctors note that patients who overcome cancer and other life-threatening diseases have one quality in common. All tend to "take charge" of their own recovery and progress. They conduct research on their medical problems, ask intelligent questions of doctors, seek second opinions, adhere strictly to dietary, medical and other health regimens, and generally maintain aggressive, positive attitudes about their eventual recovery.

There is a lesson here for Master's and doctoral students. The important point is that you must *make your thesis, dissertation or project happen.* No one else can or will. You must be unrelenting, always focused on successful completion, and methodical about the sequence of activities that lead to completion.

Be optimistic, confident and aggressive. I would like to encourage you to plunge into this book with optimism. As you read, try out the ideas introduced. For example, you should try to write one or several titles that capture the essence of what you intend in your theses or dissertation. Try one or more of the sample "organizational patterns" offered in Chapter 3, or one or more of the 21 offered in the companion book to this one----*21 Models for Developing and Writing Theses, Dissertations and Projects.*

As you develop your scholarly activity, be sure to adhere to deadlines and other requirements of your department. Remember that there are many other criteria to meet and things you must do while you write. For example, while you devise, pilot-test and mail a survey central to your thesis, you should complete an acceptable draft of the first three chapters of your document.

Let's return to the aggressive aspect of the caption above. It frequently is the case that one or more members of your committee will not give a prompt response to your proposal or, later, your first three chapters. Some might actually misplace or even *lose* your document. While this is unfair, unprofessional behavior by faculty members, it happens!

You have every right to a reaction by faculty members within a reasonable time. For this reason, you should always make a courteous follow-up inquiry about each submission. When? You should make such an inquiry as soon as you have received reactions from the other committee members.

Here is another example of the importance of an aggressive attitude. It frequently is the case that one or more members of your committee will retire or leave the university at the end of the semester or year. This is a situation that is likely to require you to adjust to the preferences, ideas and idiosyncrasies of a new committee member. In many instances, your aggressive, proactive approach can result in completion of your study before a committee change is necessary. How? By using the fact of the upcoming change as a reason for pushing forward with your study. Few committee members would argue with your right to do so!

Let's restate a point made earlier. *You* must *make* your thesis, dissertation or project happen!

It helps to realize that you are not alone, that most students experience general indecision about topics in the early stages of terminal scholarly activities. This general indecision often is accompanied by fears about the adequacy of your work and whether you will satisfy your committee. You will probably start, stop, change, and modify your ideas several times in the early going. Stick with it, and your perseverance will pay!

> *Visualize the complete title of your bound thesis or dissertation as it might appear on a library shelf. If you can "capture" your study idea in a title, you can complete the study!*

Summary:

There exist no reasons why persons who have completed M.A. or Ph.D coursework cannot move swiftly through to completion of required theses or dissertations. After all, they should be thoroughly familiar with most of the relevant related content as well as the professional opinions, biases and other predispositions of their M.A. or doctoral committee members.

The major challenge faced by each student is selection and thorough development of a topic that is (1) an original, meaningful contribution to the literature of the field; (2)

acceptable to professors of a committee of faculty members; and (3) feasible for completion within a relatively short time-span.

Students must understand that findings in theses, dissertations and projects will not *totally revolutionize* thinking in their fields. Rather, they will help to expand the knowledge base of the field with *countless small additions* to its knowledge base. Failure to understand this point leads to dilution of findings, serious limitations on generalizations, and feelings of being overwhelmed by the ambitiousness and scope of their scholarly ventures.

2

Basic Understandings Needed for Success

You have made the first step, that of solid grasp of the meaning of *useful generalizability,* the essence of all research effort. Your next step is to understand the basic steps involved in getting to that goal. This lengthy first chapter discusses those basics. Please make sure that you understand its main ideas.

There are several major related *knowledge* and *performance* competencies required for completion of terminal scholarly activities.

This chapter focuses on knowledge and performance competencies because they are prerequisites to successful completion of your terminal scholarly activities. If you completed a graduate course in research methods, it is likely that you are familiar with them. You should "brush up" on them before moving forward. Knowledge competencies are things you should *know*; and Performance competencies are things that you must *be able to do*. Equally important, the two groups are interdependent and mutually enhancing.

You must understand clearly the basic traditions of two major research communities, Quantitative and Qualitative. The first argument for clear understanding of both quantitative and qualitative rsearch methods is that you broaden your range of options for more effective research outcomes. The fortunate reality is that quantitative and qualitative approaches to research are not mutually exclusive. While each has its place in the overall scheme of research, they can be combined. You are well on your way to success in accomplishing your research goals if and when you understand the basics of both.

Second, if you arc like most graduate students, it is likely that you already understand the basic Quantitative research paradigm. You probably need to improve your background in *Qualitative* research! After all, research methods classes in most graduate schools lean toward quantitative methods, for reasons discussed later in this book. It is likely that the great majority of your professors preferred and emphasized Quantitative research.

The third and most important reason is that qualitative research can be even *more effective* than quantitative research in some cases. Why? The reason is that it promises more meaningful outcomes in the real world, *in the actual context of the problem.* Note this: several of the most important concepts, constructs and models in many fields were qualitative in origin. A few notable examples are the findings and writings of Jean Piaget, Erik Erikson, Sigmund Freud, Carl Rogers and many others whose contributions are used daily in a wide range of fields.

> Don't be misled by the popular notion that Quantitative Research is *"more scientific"* and thus more worthy. Certain studies are possible **only** through Qualitative research!

Because most persons can readily understand new concepts by comparison to known ones, we dedicate the section below to a comparison of qualitative and quantitative methods. Starting with the oft-repeated reminder that the two methods are frequently compatible within research ventures, we now look at similarities and differences.

Comparisons of Qualitative and Quantitative Research. A few distinctions between the two research methods are noteworthy:

1. Qualitative data is acquired through naturalistic, free observation made by observers with informed backgrounds, while quantitative data results from controlled *measurement* of variables derived from existent theory.

2. Qualitative research is broadly descriptive, holistic, and directed toward *discovery*, while quantitative research is relatively narrow, specific, and directed toward *"proof."*

3. Qualitative researchers try to gain in-depth understandings of social problems. By contrast, quantitative approaches typically aim to show cause-effect relationships based on prespecified variables, leading to predictions and generalizations of findings to appropriate populations.

4. Significance is conceptualized differently in the Quantitative and Qualitative research traditions. Informed judgments based on knowledge of the field constitute the

basis of conclusions of significance in *qualitative* research. Such judgments as to the significance of findings are made on the basis of whether a given finding is likely to have meaningful impact on what is already known. The process of making such judgments is enhanced by several strategies, including confirmation, structural corroboration, referential adeuacy, long-term observation and others. In *quantitative* research, one or several hypotheses are tested using appropriate statistics, followed by inferences at predetermined probabilities based on statistical outcomes.

5. Each research community relates to different notions about generalizability. Quantitative researchers relate to the concept of *representativeness*, which they believe is assured through related methods of sampling, hypothesis testing and inference to the populations from which samples are drawn. Qualitative researchers are divided about the importance of generalizability. Some dismiss it as unimportant (Denzin 1983, 133-34). Others substitute other concepts in its place (Lincoln and Guba 1985, 124). However, Schofield (1990, 201-32) notes that interest in generalizability has increased among qualitative researchers.

6. Much Qualitative research is exploratory and open to the possibility of large numbers of variables uncovered over a small number of subjects or contexts. On the other hand, Quantitative research usually looks at a small number of prespecified variables over a large number of subjects.

> *It helps to realize that many persons tend to avoid or even discount the importance of Qualitative research because it does not yield to formulas, prescriptions or "patness." However, if you're an informed observer who can "capture" and describe situations, events and contexts with rich description, you should try it!*

I hope that you will try Qualitative research. With it, you might be able to overcome most of your research problems.

Getting Started in Qualitative research. A good starting point is *Educational Criticism,* a method conceptualized by Eisner (1979, 190-260). Taken from relevant aspects of art and literary criticism, ethnography and educational evaluation, Educational Criticism is aimed at description, interpretation and evaluation (Ibid, 203-213). Readers are likely to enhance their understanding of qualitative research by reading

Eisner, Eliot W. 1979. *The Educational Imagination.* **New York: Macmillan Publishers.**

Eisner, Eliot W. 1991. *The Enlightened Eye: Qualitative Inquiry and the Enhancement of Educational Practice.* **New York: MacmillanPublishers.**

You must possess a thoroughly informed background in the literature of your field. Because of their importance, the terms *informed backgrounds* or *informed backdrops* are used repeatedly throughout this book. Whether you are developing a procedural model, a content analysis, an ethnography, a case study, or a relatively simple desk audit evaluation for an office system, you must do so from an informed background. Such a background comes from knowledge of the literature of your field as well as familiarity with daily operating contexts.

No matter what "organizational pattern" or type of study you undertake, an informed background in your field is crucial. One of the simplest patterns, Content Analysis, can serve as an example. Although examination of artifacts or historical records in quest of sustained themes seems simple, *you must make the case for doing so prior to embarking on the study.* You can only make such a case from thorough knowledge of your field of interest. Other types of studies, such as those based on ethnographies and case studies, are much more challenging. Why? They require even greater in-depth understanding of what is relevant in your field of interest. How can a linguist studying Chicano dialects do so without knowledge of normative Hispanic dialects? Similarly, how can an *uninformed* observer of teaching evaluate the performance of a group of teachers in a study?

Within the proposal written to your Master's or doctoral committee, you will have to present and defend the case for your proposed study. How can you make such an excellent presentation and vigorous defense without an informed background on the topic in question?

You must be able to see analogies and distinctions between your study interests and existent research. Some readers will experience few if any problems in coming up with titles for their theses, dissertations, or projects. Others will perceive the task of generating a workable title as a major obstacle, even to the extent of giving up and abandoning the quest for an advanced degree. For this second group, use of analogy between your research interest and one or more existent studies might be useful.

Suppose your preliminary research in the area of school finance shows an unattractive trend towards regressive taxation for schools in the several midwestern states, a trend that overburdens those least able to pay. You have seen an example of a dissertation entitled, *An Analysis of Recent Educational Finance Trends in Selected Western States, 1980-1990.* There is absolutely nothing wrong with using the topic, *Trends Toward Regressive Taxation in Educational Finance in Selected Midwestern States, 1990-1995*, provided:

1. Your thorough research has ruled out the possibility of an identical study.

2. Such a study can be "sold" to your thesis or dissertation committee.

Furthermore, added in-depth investigation of that earlier study is likely to reveal various avenues and options for overcoming problems in your study----and there is nothing wrong with using that information!

If possible, try these steps:

1. Start with a title. I am a firm believer in capturing the essence of what you are trying to do in your title. There is nothing shameful about writing many, even dozens, of would-be titles in the interest of finally settling on one that "captures" the major points involved in your study. As you write several titles, it is important to remember that *useful generalizability* is the long-range desired end of all theses and dissertations. Simply bearing in mind your generalization target will work wonders for your ability to finalize a title.

The title of your study should be as succinct as possible, never longer than 16 words in length. It should name the population studied, include the relationship between variables studied, and above all, avoid redundancy.

2. After tentatively deciding on a title, do your best to narrow its breadth without losing the critically important element of generalizability. Overambitiousness in topic selection is one of the major problems I have experienced with students through the years. You should not expect findings of your thesis or dissertation to *totally revolutionize* thinking in your field. Instead, those findings typically contribute to the expansion of the knowledge base of your field by adding a relatively small amount of new knowledge. Remember also that it is neither possible nor desirable to write about *every* aspect of a problem nor area of study.

3. Select an "organizational pattern" that seems to offer the best avenue to your research interest. Many organizational patterns (thesis types for use as developmental frameworks) are available in the companion volume to this one. That volume, entitled *21 Models for Developing and Writing Dissertations, Theses and Projects,* is available from the same source as this book.

4. Write an exploratory "skeletal" three chapters that adhere to the general outline offered in Chapter 4. A "skeletal" three chapters uses simple, basic language with no elaboration. Write strictly to the caption requirements. Remember, you are simply trying to determine whether the "organizational pattern" helps to "capture" what you have in mind!

Use the basic framework for a thesis or dissertation offered in Chapter 4 and strive to write within the meaning of each caption while adhering to the "organizational pattern" selected. Please note that some captions might not be appropriate or relevant to the topic you select. If so, omit them.

> *Good writers are made, not born!   The more you write, the*
> *better you write!   Get started, write freely, then edit cautiously.*

You must be able to choose and execute a research design appropriate to your chosen "organizational pattern." The research design chosen must be appropriate to the "organizational pattern" chosen. This should not be difficult, for many organizational patterns will virtually suggest certain research designs.

Perhaps it is simply human nature, but many students learn about and develop preferences for certain research designs or even certain statistics during their research methods and statistics classes. Frequently, they attempt to incorporate these preferences into their research whether they are appropriate or not. Even worse, they think *only* of those problems and solutions that they can resolve with their preferred research designs or statistics.

You must also avoid another similar tendency. An example of it is a student preference for, say, quantitative research designs at the exclusion of qualitative aspects. In such cases, the "tail is wagging the dog," because choices that should *follow* choice of a problem precede problem choice. It is obvious that such "cart before the horse" thinking destroys chances for conducting meaningful research.

What does this mean for you? The answer is that at this point, think *only* of the problems you are trying to solve, the intended generalizability, your "hunches" about causes and solutions, and the best "organizational pattern" for getting started toward a solutions to those problems.

Those "hunches" related to problems you are trying to solve actually form the bases of hypotheses. Hypotheses are important guideposts that direct research and form the bases for evaluating research outcomes.

Formulating and using hypotheses. It is best to think of hypotheses in broad terms, involving several definitions. Unfortunately, the most common definition found in most current research and statistics textbooks carries the notion that hypotheses must be *testable* with and only with statistics at established levels of certainty. This is both untrue and limiting.

On the contrary, hypotheses are assumptions made for the sake of argument and subsequent investigation. You can investigate them both quantitatively and qualitatively.

In quantitative research, most of the hypotheses testing activity focuses on determination of the likelihood that a particular sample could have originated from a population with a hypothesized characteristic. The null hypothesis, used for hypothesis testing, always makes a claim about a single numerical value, and is tested using the sampling distribution of the statistic chosen. Sampling distributions indicate minimum values required in order to justify a conclusion of an improbable occurrence, leading to rejection of the null hypothesis.

In qualitative research, hypotheses are *examined* (and *supported* or *not supported*.), not *tested.* Let's look at the example of a fictitious thesis entitled, *A Qualitative Examination of the Causes of Bulimia in American Female Adolescents.* Perhaps the researcher hypothesized that one characteristic typical of bulimia sufferers is role confusion due to inconsistent parental rule-enforcing behaviors. The Case Study method used in such a thesis to examine, say, 12 to 15 girls in great detail might fail to support that hypothesis and suggest other causes instead.

Here are two more important observations about hypotheses:

1. Hypotheses should be formulated in ways that ensure that they can be tested or examined, depending on the research approach involved.

2. The worthiness of hypotheses should be defensible. This means that you cannot pluck hypotheses from thin air. You should have a definite basis for selecting one or more hypotheses. Such reasons can derive from your previous research or from the research of others.

You must understand the types, uses, strengths and limitations of models. Let's start by restating a point made earlier, that *all* theses and dissertations are models. Some are explicit models, others are implicit. The dissertation example given in Chapter 1, *A Validated Curriculum Alignment Procedure for Mathematics Curricula, 1-6,* is an explicit model. A thesis entitled *Characteristic Career Paths of Successful Female Hispanic Hospital Administrators* is an example of an implicit model. The important point here is that both can guide practice in many similar contexts.

A model should be an example worthy of imitation (Kaplan 1964, 258) A model or paradigm is also a representation that summarizes data neatly and aids understanding (Lippitt 1973; Zais 1976). The dissertation in the preceding paragraph resulted in a model usable by persons organizing mathematics curricula. The thesis above implies that it contains a model that shows how to use sign language in teaching second language learners.

Those of you who are still searching for a thesis or dissertation topic should explore the need for models in your field. Virtually all fields beg for models that help with tasks ranging from improving conceptual grasp to step-by-step procedures. For example, the field of Education is still in need of better approaches to teaching reading. Universities continue to grapple with better ways of evaluating junior professors. Public agencies are always under pressure for improving delivery of various services.

Types, uses and strengths of models. There are many kinds of models. Although a theory is of itself a model, our interest in this book centers on models that can be translated into behaviors for humans. Names of model types frequently are confusing (See Kaplan [1964, 273-74] or Zais [1976, 92-93]). Other writers offer even more names and groupings.

We can avoid some of this confusion by describing models in terms of their basic functions. Those functions are:

1. *Data organization*, leading to neat summation of ideas, often helping us to "capture" and understand complex interrelationships and dynamics.

2. *Reduction of uncertainty* during transmission of scientific and other challenging, sophisticated ideas, by

a. Clarifying and simplifying relationships among concepts.

b. Helping to prioritize propositions in order of their importance.

c. Revealing knowledge gaps.

d. Broadening the concept of measurement to include qualitative aspects.

e. Reduction of vagueness in transmission of qualitative concepts.

Limitations of models. Many writers have identified several shortcomings of models as well as several tendencies they invite in their users. In sum, those writers contend that use and overuse of models leads to several problems. These problems are *extremes* and *erroneous tendencies*. Typical extremes are overgeneralization, logical fallacies, overemphasis on symbols, overemphasis on form, oversimplification, and overemphasis on rigor. The erroneous tendencies are equally dangerous. One is the tendency to make the model fit the situation, and the other is the tendency to view the model as an accurate representation of reality.

Building and using models. Any model that you build must contain three important ingredients: recognizable structural elements, a working relationship between these elements, and definite processes. These ingredients are especially important for those of you who are interested in thesis or dissertation ideas similar to many of the examples offered throughout this book.

Gage (1978, 87) identified a model called the "process-product paradigm." His model is relevant for many of the studies discussed in this book because of the relationship between process and outcome. You can apply this "process-product paradigm" to many study ideas in this book.

For clarity, let's discuss this in the context of the dissertation mentioned earlier, *A Validated Curriculum Alignment Procedure for Mathematics Curricula, 1-6.* This model was built by searching for "processes" (activities, conditions and commonalities) that predict and result in "products" (In this case, a successful mathematics curriculum that satisfies required conditions of continuity, articulation and balance, as well as teacher usability).

The "process-product" model is especially useful because:

1. It is based on long and short-range goals (the aligned curriculum and higher achievement resulting from teacher unity of purpose).

2. It identifies internal and external forces related to the goal (teacher consensus building, teacher meetings, goal prioritization).

3. It identifies constraints or barriers to goal achievement (negative attitudes, teacher resistance to change, bargained schedules).

4. It shows the connection between the goal and system resources (teacher released time, inservice costs, materials, supplies, consultants).

Understanding models in the context of this book. You should understand that this book uses a broader definition of the term *model* than that typically used in most discussions, especially those in behavioral sciences. Unfortunately, in some behavioral fields the term *model* is so over-intellectualized and abstract as to destroy the usefulness of models.

Models are Tools. Models are tools, first and foremost. They are tools that help us to understand, organize, proceed, evaluate or a combination thereof. A curriculum plan for teaching reading is a model. Such a curriculum plan helps teachers to (1) *understand* long-range goals, (2) *organize* an upcoming series of lessons, and (3) *evaluate* learning after passage of time. A standard procedure for maintaining adequate levels in various watersheds in a utility district is a model. A board-adopted long-range strategy for holding an industry sales position is a model. A bargained procedure for evaluating city employees is a model. At a smaller, personal level, each principal who evaluates teachers must have a personalized conception (Conceptual Model) of good or effectiveteaching.

Avoid confusion about models. You must learn to recognize and avoid the confusion brought about by terms used in discussion of models. In many studies, you use a model to derive another model. Although nothing is inherently wrong with that, it is confusing.

Two "organizational patterns" are offered as examples later in this Chapter. Please understand that each organizational pattern is a model. In *21 Organizational Patterns for Developing and Completing Your Thesis, Dissertation or Project*, the companion book to this one, several of the organizational patterns offer various kinds of models as the hoped-for outcomes of studies. Remember, also, that you can combine certain model types.

Since there are many types of models as well as model names, we will limit our discussion below to the kinds of models used and referred to in this book. Models referred to in this book are *Conceptual*, *Evaluative*, *Procedural*, and *Developmental*. Many of the models in this book combine characteristics of one or more of these four. Each type deserves discussion.

Conceptual models. Please understand that all models are conceptual models because they help us to visualize, discern, grasp notions, ideate, and most importantly, to organize our ideas. For example, the organizational patterns offered later in this Chapter are *Conceptual* models. Why? The answer is that each organizational pattern provides an overall framework for conceptualizing, organizing, and presenting your thesis or dissertation.

Please note, also, that the *Evaluative, Procedural,* and *Developmental* models explained below are Conceptual models as well. Although each one has a specific function, they also help us to organize our ideas and develop personal *Gestalts* about what we see.

You need to pause momentarily and consider the important distinction between these organizational patterns as conceptual models and any other conceptual model you might want to develop. For example, you might want to develop a curricular framework for incorporation of relevant Hispanic-American history events into 12th grade American History books and curricular materials. You might want to derive an experience-based curricular framework by conducting a large random survey of high schools with large Hispanic populations. You could use the *Profiles of Effective Practices* organizational pattern as the basic conceptual model for organizing your study. However, if you want to know *how* these high schools organized their programs, you could also use the *Experience-Based Procedural Model* organizational pattern. The combination of elements in the two approaches should yield what you want. (The "organizational patterns" discussed here and elsewhere in this book are featured in *21 Organizational Patterns for Developing and Completing Your Thesis, Dissertation or Project,* available from the same sources as this book).

Many of the organizational patterns that use qualitative methods are *Conceptual* models as well. They fit that definition because they, too, are ways of conceptualizing and gaining clear pictures of possible studies. Examples of these are *Content Analyses, Historical Co-Occurrences, Behavioral*

Co-Occurrences, Cases for or Against, Case Studies, and *Literary Analyses.*

Evaluative models. These are models or frameworks that you use to assess or evaluate something, some phenomena in your field. The organizational patterns or conceptual models that fit neatly into this category are *Broad-Based Assessments, Group Attitude Profiles, Profiles of Dominant Practices, Comparative Analyses,* and *Analyses of Trends.* You should note that certain qualitative studies have evaluative interests as well. Among these are *Studies of Notable Qualities of Effective Performers, Studies of Notable Qualities of Effective Contexts,* and *Role Examinations.* Remember that you can and should combine these organizational patterns when possible.

Procedural models. As the name indicates, these are models that present definite, well-sequenced steps for accomplishing certain important tasks in various fields. Examples of these in this book are *Experience-Based Procedural Models* and *Validated Procedural Models.* Both depend on consensus of successful practitioners for fashioning the ultimate outcome, the model. You could also refer to each as *consensus-based* models.

Developmental models. These models present *ways of developing* various products, like curricular frameworks, resource directories, manuals, management systems and others. You should not confuse them with the actual projects, manuals and other products discussed in Chapter 21. In that Chapter, our interests are the products themselves, not ways of developing them!

Two organizational patterns in this book focus on developmental models as hoped-for outcomes. One is the *Validated Procedural Model*, an operational paradigm that must be proven in practice. The other is *Prototype Development*, an organizational pattern that uses consensus to develop a first-of-its-kind solution to a problem plaguing a field.

Remember combinations! When conceptualizing and choosing your study, you should remember possible combinations of organizational patterns. The possibilities are so plentiful that they defy description and thorough discussion in the space possible here. The message here is clear: combine organizational patterns when possible!

You must be able to choose statistical and other specific data handling methods appropriate to a chosen research design. Choice of appropriate statistical tests is a process involving three decisions. The three-decision process is quite simple. In order, decisions have to be made related to (1) Level of measurement, (2) number of groups, and (3) nature of the groups, or number of categories when only one group is involved (in Nominal data).

In-depth discussion of choice of statistical tests is a matter that is beyond the purposes of this book. However, the procedure is simple and anyone can master it. The process of choosing statistical tests, complete with a "road map," is discussed in an admirably straightforward manner in

Sharp, Vicki F. 1979. *Statistics for the Social Sciences*. Boston: Little, Brown.

In the initial stages of formulating your study, it is important to remember that choice of a title comes first, followed by selection of an appropriate research design. Choice of a statistical test follows selection of your research design.

My students frequently question the need for in-depth study and understanding of statistics, since statistical packages are readily available in software programs. Why, they ask, must they understand the inner workings of, say, the Chi Square function or Analysis of Variance? My answer is always the same. When you understand the derivation of certain statistics, you improve your understanding and conceptual grasp of research outcomes.

You should review the following basic statistical concepts before moving forward:

Frequency distributions and their uses.
Statistical notation.
Measures of central tendency.
Measures of dispersion.
Standard scores.
Normal distributions.
Normalized standard score distributions
Pearson Product Moment Correlation.
Other correlation coefficients.
Principles of prediction.
Statistical procedures in measurement.
Basic probability theory.
Basic sampling theory.
Statistical hypotheses and hypothesis testing error.
Non-parametric tests: Mann-Whitney *U*, Wilcoxon, Kolmogorov, Kolmogorov-Smirnov, the Chi-Square Distribution and Chi-Square tests.
Parametric tests: *t* - test I, *t* -test II, the *F* - distribution, Simple ANOVA and Multiple Comparisons, Two-Way ANOVA, ANCOVA, and Multiple Regression.

You must be able to apply the basic principles of survey research, including administration, analysis, and drawing conclusions therefrom. The most serious and common problem in survey research deserves discussion first. That problem derives from the tendency of many researchers to obtain data from randomly or arbitrarily drawn samples and present the findings as absolutely and certainly representative of parent populations. This is a dangerous tendency that results in misrepresentation and, often, exaggerationof fact. This tendency is so common in survey research that I decided to add the brief section below, *An important cautionary note related to surveys.*

Although in-depth discussion of survey research is outside the purposes of this book, a brief sidebar about them might be profitable here. A survey is a method of obtaining data from a sample of persons who are representative of the population to which they belong. Surveys have many purposes, ranging from presidential poll predictions to market analysis. Some focus on characteristics or behaviors like eating habits, sexual preferences, spending patterns and the like. Others focus on opinions and attitudes. Still others combine questions, including both types.

The central interest of surveys is getting at the behaviors, attitudes and opinions mentioned above. Another interest is demographic. Specifically, much survey research concerns the *co-occurrence* of behaviors, attitudes and opinions with other factual information like gender, age, education levels attained, marital status, occupation, place of residence, type of school, type of hospital, type of law practice, size of city, and others. This means that demographic questions are often as important as substantive ones in survey research.

You can conduct surveys in a variety of ways: by telephone, by mail, or in person-to-person interviews. Each avenue has its advantages and disadvantages. For example, while mailed surveys (questionnaires) have advantages of privacy, cost effectiveness, low staffing needs, and relatively quick turnaround, they have the disadvantages of lack of flexibility, closed-end responses, and reliance on reading comprehension skills. On the other hand, telephone and in-person interviews carry the advantages of flexibility, open-ended responses, and clarification when necessary.

The complete survey process involves:

1. Determining the specific, unambiguous objectives of the survey.

2. Carefully evaluating the feasibility of a survey for obtaining the necessary data.

3. Deciding on the mode of data collection (telephone, mail, or in-person).

4. Planning the questionnaire, incorporating adherence to specifications, concepts of interest, scope, language and phraseology, length, order of questions, and appearance of the questionnaire. Other planning factors are subtler, including minimization of respondent bias, sensitivity of content, extent of reliance on memory, and others.

5. Identifying the sample.

6. Scheduling the survey, including considerations of time required.

7. Collecting the survey data, using standardized procedures that insure that questions are presented to respondents in the same way.

A cautionary note related to surveys. Many researchers make erroneous conclusions about the nature and makeup of the populations they study. Most of the time, this happens when they ignore or fail to account for possible significant differences between obtained samples and their populations.

When we survey a sample group (which we *can* know precisely), we are trying to understand and make inferences about characteristics of the population (which we *cannot* know precisely). Since the sample is only a small proportion of its population, there is a strong possibility that random differences will exist between sample and population characteristics. For example, when a sample reveals that respondents are 47 percent male and 53 percent female, we have no assurances that the same percentages of males and females exist in the population. Why? Because the *one sample we happened to draw* might have had more females (or males) than existed in the population. Thus, in spite of all of our attempts at random sampling and assuring representativeness of the sample, the sheer luck of the draw might result in a non-representative sample!

Because of this problem inherent in sampling, much of the central concern of the field of statistics is about estimating the characteristics of the population. For example, reputable researchers who conduct, say, presidential election polls must be able to speak of the probability that findings related to characteristics in the obtained sample are similar to corresponding characteristics in the population. A second related concern is *hypothesis testing*, or determination of whether relationships between variables found in surveys exist as such in the population.

All of this means that researchers who use surveys in their studies should familiarize themselves with the *techniques of inference* for survey data. This involves many concerns. Among these are sample design, sample types, purposeful sampling, sample size, sampling error, measurement error, response rates, respondent and interviewer effects, induced bias, standard error estimation, confidence intervals, weighting schemes, and even seasonal adjustments wherever applicable.

Let's take just one of these concerns----sample size----and illustrate its importance here. Sample size (and response rate, mentioned above) is critically important to deriving useful information from surveys. Why? Because the accuracy of inferences made from sample to population are directly related to and dependent on sample size.

An example will help you to understand this *extremely important* point. Suppose you are trying to sample the (approximately) 2,000 kindergarten teachers in your state, in the interest of determining their teaching preferences, specifically whether they prefer skill-based or holistic approaches to teaching language. Let's say that your sample returns indicated that 58 percent preferred skill-based approaches. How sure can you be that the same percentage (of skills-based teachers) is true in the total population of kindergarten teachers?

The answer is that you can never be *absolutely* sure, but with a sample of adequate size, it would be possible to be highly confident that the sample is representative of the population. In the kindergarten teacher survey example, with at least 322 returns you could be 95 percent confident that 58 percent of the population of kindergarten teachers preferred skills-based approaches, with 5 percent sampling error. With only 188 returns, you could be (only) 85 percent confident that your sample was a true reflection of the population, again, with a 5 percent sampling error factor.

Although space considerations prohibit presentation of statistical details related to sampling size determination, there is nothing difficult about it. One of the best treatments of sampling and sampling size determination can be found in

Longmore, M.A., Dunn, D., and Jarboe, G.R. 1996.
The Survey Research Project Manual.
Minneapolis: West Publishing.

Persons interested in survey research should acquire this valuable book, cited again in Chapter 4.

Questionnaires, the information-gathering tools of surveys. Although in-depth discussion of questionnaires is beyond the purposes and scope of this book, a few observations about them might be useful. Let's start with the observation that there is nothing really difficult about questionnaires. Design of effective questionnaires is largely a matter of common sense and unwavering attention to the information you want. It is a good idea to arm yourself with as much information as possible about effective questionnaire design. Here are a few excellent references:

Berdie, D.R., and Anderson, J.F. 1974. *Questionnaires:*
***Design and Use.* Metuchen, N.J.: Scarecrow Press.**

Fowler, F.J. 1993. *Survey Research Methods.* Applied
Social Research Methods Series, Vol. 1.
Newbury Park, CA: Sage Publications.

Rossi, P.H., Wright, J.D., and Anderson, A.B. 1983.
Handbook of Survey Research.
San Diego: Academic Press.

Schuman, H., and Presser, S. 1981. *Questions and Answers*
in Attitude Surveys: Experiments on Question Form, Wording
***and Context.* New York: Academic Press.**

Sudman, S., and Bradbburn, N.M. 1982. *Asking Questions.* San Francisco: Jossey-Bass.

Vockell, E.L., and Asher, J.W. 1995. *EducationalResearch.* Englewood Cliffs, N.J.: Prentice-Hall.

You should note a few principles and main points about questionnaires that should be mentioned here, together with things that should be avoided. All questionnaires should (1) be based on definite hypotheses; (2) be cleared of ambiguities and confusing terms by pretesting; (3) guarantee confidentiality; (4) be as short as possible; (5) have items arranged in a logical sequence; (6) use language appropriate for respondents; and (7) use item formats appropriate to the information sought.

A few more aspects are noteworthy about questionnaires. You enjoy tremendous advantages by using scaled response formats (like the Likert continuum) in two common survey research situations. The first is whenever you need to clarify distributions of group preferences on opinions or attitudes. The second is when you must make statistical comparisons.

Items should be grouped on the basis of intended uses. An example is Part I (about the respondent), Part II (about the context), and Part III (the central research interest). When questionnaires are sent to respondents, the transmittal letter should (1) include an introductory statement that identifies the sender, (2) request a response to the questionnaire, and (3) explain the value of the response, including how it will be used and how much time it should take.

When you design questionnaires, make sure you avoid:

1. The assumption that surveys can lead to causal inferences.

2. The assumption that the answers of respondents will always be accurate.
3. Questions that are not important or relevant to the information sought.
4. Confusing, ambiguous terms that are open to various interpretations.
5. Terms not common to the interest area.
6. Questions with popular desirability.
7. Items worded in ways that influence respondents in the direction of one response over another.
8. Confusion about different requirements for *opinion* surveys and *attitude* measures (Anastasi 1968, 479-82).

We will wrap up this section with two reminders. The first is a powerful caution: sending questionnaires to your sample group is like scrambling eggs: you can only do it once. This means that before you send it, you should exercise extreme care to (1) insure that your questionnaire is valid, that it will get the information it is designed to get; (2) see that it is economical in response time required; and (3) see that it is generally usable. The second thing to remember is that you should continue working on the first three chapters of your thesis or dissertation *while* you develop and administer your questionnaire. Doing so will result in considerable time savings. The processes of pretesting, refining, mailing, waiting for responses, follow-up mailing and waiting for more responses take time.

You must be able to apply the principles of effective scholarly writing. Like several other topics, the principles of scholarly writing are frequently overlooked in books dedicated to development of theses, dissertations and projects. In light of this shortcoming in the literature, a few paragraphs about the nature of scholarly writing seem appropriate.

Understanding scholarly writing and argument. Scholarly writing is *expository* in nature. Its basic purpose is explanation, although it may employ various devices, including description, argument, or narration. It is important to realize that persuasion is *not* the central purpose of scholarly writing. Rather, it seeks to explain solutions to intellectual problems.

You must always direct scholarly writing to serious readers. Such readers are persons who (1) usually are knowledgeable about many aspects of the subject, and who (2) have certain expectations about procedures and requirements that must be followed in the body of the text.

Scholarly writing *must* contain the elements *analysis, presentation of evidence* and *careful logical argument*, all offered within the framework of language characteristic of your field. Each element deserves elaboration.

Analysis is a basic expectation of scholarly writing. It is so important that the format of virtually all theses, dissertations, or projects produced anywhere *require* a major section or even a chapter (Chapter 4 or 5, usually) dedicated to it. Effective analysis demands exploration of reasons for phenomena observed in a study.

Presentation of evidence in scholarly writing requires provision of supporting evidence for each conclusion or opinion expressed by the writer. You should offer each bit of supporting evidence immediately after a conclusion or opinion. Doing so improves narrative continuity and reader recognition of the basis of the total argument that might be offered later. You should present *both* supporting and opposing evidence. In other words, you must present evidence that appears to refute the main argument *during* the argument. Presentation of rival hypotheses and theories in this manner actually strengthens your case!

Careful Reasoned Argument in Scholarly Writing. *Careful reasoned argument* is a process that leads to a definite conclusion. In combination, the reasoning processes and resultant conclusions build and shape the overall argument of the thesis or dissertation in sequences that are logical to informed readers.

Ways of Supporting Reasoned Argument. You can use several supports to careful reasoned argument in scholarly writing. Many are useful elsewhere in scholarly arguments. However, they are extremely useful in Chapter 5 of theses and dissertations, during reasoned arguments. They are:

1. Citing *Confirmation,* a process of supporting or disconfirming evidence through several means. Perhaps the most important is an internal check that involves a search for consistent evidence in the data record. Of course, a simultaneous check for evidence that disconfirms evidence is equally important. Confirmation in careful reasoned argument helps to emphasize the consistency of the evidence.

2. Citing *Triangulation,* an analytical technique involving comparison of data collected from several vantage points. The strength of triangulation is cancellation of methodological bias. Reasoned argument in quantitative studies uses triangulation to "sell" the accuracy of information, while in qualitative studies reasoned

argument uses triangulation to broaden the base of evidence that contributes to more meaningful analyses.

3. Citing *long-term observation,* repeated observations and data gathered about the same phenomena over a long period of time, an argument on behalf of the validity of findings (Merriam 1988, 169). Arguments and conclusions based on many long-term observations and their revelations help to sell the belief that details of social phenomena are fully revealed and clear to investigators. The same is true of the contextual circumstances in which these details have meaning.

4. Citing *comparisons to established standards or criteria.* When and if an established standard exists, you have a basis for making a reasonably reliable case for the comparability of two or more contexts. These citations are particularly useful when making arguments about the intended generalizability of research outcomes. Accreditation agency criteria, guidelines of professional organizations, and state evaluative criteria are examples of established criteria.

5. Focusing on *analogies and similarities* of participants while making a case for *Population Validity.* Population validity is the degree to which participants included in a study are equivalent to, or representative of, others in similar contexts. When possible in planning a study, researchers must identify the groups about which they want to draw conclusions. When you present reasoned arguments for the external validity of findings, you should cite detailed similarities between study group members and the population group.

6.   Focusing on *analogies and similarities* of *contexts*
while making a case for *Setting Validity*. You can make
a case for Setting Validity by focusing on the similarity
of the setting of your study and others in similar
contexts. When planning a study, you must describe
clearly the settings to which you want to generalize.

Don't overlook plain old **commonsense** *when presenting
reasoned argument! Remember that some things are simply
face-evident.*

Avoiding Logical Fallacies in Reasoned Argument.
It is important to avoid certain logical fallacies in reasoned
argument. Most are superficially logical, and actually detract
from the effectiveness of scholarly argument. The most
common logical fallacies are:

1. *Begging the question,* frequently referred to as circular
   reasoning.
2.   The *post hoc* fallacy, confusing precedence with
   causality.
3. *Either-or* reasoning, the assumption that there are only
   two sides to a given question.
4. *False assertion of a claim,* making a claim without
   reasoned support.
5. *Over-reliance on authority,* the assumption that a fact,
   event or occurrence reported by an expert is true, while
   ignoring contrary evidence.
6. *Oversimplification,* giving easy answers to complicated
   problems.

7. *Slanting,* selective inclusion of supportive evidence and exclusion or minimizing opposing evidence.

One of the best treatments of the essentials and principles of reasoned argument can be found in

Meehan, E.J. 1981. *Reasoned Argument inSocial Science* Westport, CT: Greenwood Press.

In scholarly writing, you should avoid:

1. Informal languagesimilar to that found in newspapers or magazines.
2. Slang and colloquialisms typical of conversations.
3. Contractions.
4. Abbreviations unless they are accepted conventions in your field.

Finally, effective scholarly writing requires ability to use languagecharacteristic of your own field. Most of you will have thought this through by now. Still, it seems important to remind you that each field of endeavor has its characteristic language, its "in" expressions and its definitions that are more or less taken for granted by those who have devoted their professional lives to a specific sphere of interest. All of this means that you must remember to modify the basic language to those conventions accepted in your field.

Summary

While theses and dissertations are significant contributions to knowledge within a field, they also are used by colleges and universities as indicators of student ability to conduct and present accurate research in a scientific, scholarly manner. Consistent with the major aims of science, their dual interests are explanation and prediction.

Generalizability can be thought of as the hoped-for end of research activity. Without it, most of research activity yields what one writer called "isolated curiosities" which promise few meaningful contributions to the knowledge base of a field.

There are several major related *knowledge* and *performance* competencies required for completion of terminal scholarly activities. Students must display:

1. Clear understanding of the basic traditions of research in two major research communities, Quantitative and Qualitative.   Additionally,   students   must   realize   that approaches in the two research traditions are not mutually exclusive, that elements are both are important in research.

2. An *informed* background in the literature of your field. It is possible to argue that this is the first and most important requirement for effective research.

3. Ability to use analogy in selecting an "organizational pattern" applicable to your own context.

4. Ability to choose and execute a research design appropriate to a chosen "organizational pattern."

5. Ability to apply the basic principles of survey research, including administration, analysis, and drawing conclusions therefrom.

6. Ability to present reasoned scholarly arguments.

7. Ability to use effective language characteristic of your own field.

3

THE COMMONSENSE OF SELECTING TOPICS FOR THESES, DISSERTATIONS OR PROJECTS

Let's face it, you bought this book because you are interested in finishing your thesis, dissertation or project as quickly as possible. That concern alone is in the realm of common sense, so you are on the right track. This chapter continues that commonsense theme by focusing on several overlooked things. Those overlooked things are items that you will not find in the literature. However, they are concerns that Master's and doctoral candidates would do well to think about as they embark on their terminal scholarly activities.

You must consider three commonsense aspects when choosing a topic for your thesis, dissertation or project: feasibility of completion within time available, access to research contexts, and support of your committee.

Strangely, students are more likely to fail to complete terminal scholarly activities for commonsense reasons than any others. The first uncompromising commonsense reality you must confront is whether the timeline of your life permits certain kinds of research. If you are like most students, you are operating on a fairly short timespan beyond which you cannot afford to continue in a master's or doctoral program.

This means that you must exclude or rule out certain topics that might exceed the timespan on which you planned your advanced degree study. Let's look at an example. Suppose an M.A. candidate has one year remaining to complete a thesis. Her interest is the impact of leadership style on productivity in computer hardware production. Two possible topics can illustrate differences in time requirements. The first topic she considered was *A Statistical Comparison of the Effects of Leadership Style in Three Computer Hardware Production Contexts.* Completing the research for a thesis like this would involve

1. Identification of three distinctly different leadership styles of existent managers in computer manufacturing.
2. A pretest of three different production situations to insure comparability.
3. Monitoring manufacturing processes in all three situations.
4. Posttesting, using numbers of serviceable units produced as an outcome criterion.
5. Statistical comparisons of outcomes.
6. Assessment of the impact of leadership style on outcomes.

Her second tentative topic was *Leadership Style and Computer Hardware Production: A Causal-Comparative Study.* Accomplishing this thesis would involve

1. Random selection of employees of three separate manufacturing units for responses to an opinnionaire

designed to determine or approximate the leadership style of their supervisors or managers.

2. Looking "backward" through productivity records of each manufacturing unit over, say, a one- or two-year interval during which all three managers were in charge.

3. Statistical comparisons of productivity figures which *have occurred already.*

4. Conclusions related to the impact of leadership styles as originally planned.

The one advantage of the first study was the likelihood of establishment of causal relationships between managerial style and productivity. However, two negatives might offset this advantage. It would (1) take much more time to complete, and (2) carry certain dangers of attrition and control that could threaten completion of the study. That is to say that the evaluation of the performances of each group could occur only over a significant timespan. Equally important, many other variables could threaten the overall validity of the study. Among them is employee turnover that would threaten the comparability of the groups and changes in manufacturing procedures and methods over which students have little or no control. On the other hand, the data in the second study have already occurred and it is readily available in the records of the company. The only remaining problem was determination of leadership style, readily available through an employee opinionnaire.

Alternatives that reduce the time required. As suggested above, there are serious *practical* consequences involved in choices of topics and the research approaches they necessitate. Put simply, certain research designs consume more time and energy than others. If you gain practical understanding of research design, you will be able to apply common sense to the evaluation of various designs *in light of your time and resources* for designing and completing your study. In other words, I would like to see you design an effective study, execute it, write it up, and then----to use a popular expression----take the money and run! The alternatives below should be considered before you finalize a research design.

Consider non-experimental research instead of experimental research. You should be very cautious about choosing *experimental* research. You might feel pressured into some variation of experimental research because many, perhaps most, faculty committee members prefer it. However, students must realize the complexities and problems involved in completing it in real-world contexts.

Let's use classroom experimental research as an example. In many if not most cases, students met with major problems when they tried to carry out their experiments. Why? It is extremely hard to maintain experimental controls in most real-world situations, especially in public school classrooms. Many things compete with the control desired. For instance, random assignment of children to classes is virtually impossible, because of competing concerns like (unattractive) teacher preferences for certain children, collective bargaining class size requirements, and other "political" considerations.

Control----of teacher time, student engaged time, consistency of methods and other variables necessary to maintain experimental integrity----is difficult, because most graduate students have no real "clout" in school contexts. Even when you overcome the initial problems, others crop up: teachers fail to adhere to or give adequate time to specific methods; or student mobility is so great that pretest-posttest analysis is virtually impossible.

Because of these "human" problems, experimental research is frequently difficult to sustain. An attractive alternative is non-experimental research.

The *Causal-Comparative* research method, called *ex post facto* research, is a direct alternative to experimental research. In this approach, inferences about variables are made solely from concomitant variation of independent and dependent variables (Kerlinger 1973, 379). In Causal-Comparative research, you collect data *after* the events have occurred. You find a situation that exists and then search back through the data for logical causal factors (Isaac and Michael 1981, 50-51). This means that Master's and doctoral students in search of sources of original research have only to (1) identify some situation that exists in their field of interest, (2) put forth one or several highly logical hypotheses about *why* that situation exists, and (3) search backward through existent data for possible causes, relationships and their meanings.

The great advantage of these research methods is that the data (a) have already occurred or (b) it is readily available, without the risks inherent in lengthy, extended experiments. However, it is important to note two more advantages. One is the obvious relative ease of retrieving and working with existent data. There is another important advantage of this type of research. It can sometimes satisfy some of the expectations of those chairpersons and committee members who insist on quantification in all research. Correspondingly, the primary disadvantage of these research methods is that you cannot make a valid claim for causal relationships between occurrences and consequences.

The most obvious approaches to non-experimental research are Historical, Descriptive, Developmental, Case and Field, Correlational, and Causal-Comparative (Ex-Post Facto). You should note that some of the most important findings in the behavioral sciences resulted, primarily, through non-experimental research. Piaget's Cognitive Development model and Erik Erikson's Personality Development model are prime examples.

Three fictitious theses (in three different fields) that could use this approach are:

Education:

Speed of Second Language Acquisition of Hispanic Bilingual Students as Related to Birth Order

Public Administration:

Education Levels of Large City Managers as Determinants of Their Attitudes Toward Public Employee Bargaining

Business:

Retraining Adaptability of Tool-and-Die Specialists as Related to Years of Experience in the Trade

---

Causal-Comparative Research is one of the most potentially productive yet overlooked research avenues. Explore it now!

The most important point to note in each example is *that the data exists already*. After the (obvious) relationships have been hypothesized *as reflected in the titles*, the only tasks that remain are: (a) determining a method of defining and categorizing the consequence, and (b) searching the data for the existence and extent of hypothesized causal factors. In example (1) above, carrying out the study would involve two steps. The first would be determining the family birth order of individual Hispanic bilingual students (who may be well into or through high school or beyond at the time of the study). The second would be analyzing the language acquisition behavior of each student, as manifested through cumulative folders, teacher opinions and other documented sources. With large enough numbers of students, patterns are likely to emerge. Also with large numbers, various correlations are possible, although it should be emphasized here that mere correlations cannot be interpreted as causal relationships between entry ages and school behavior.

Why not take advantage of research where the events on which the data are based have already occurred? Why risk the possibility of lost time, subjects dropping out, changes in procedures and many other negatives that could result in major setbacks in progress toward theses or dissertations?

Consider qualitative research. Qualitative research, discussed in Chapter 2, offers several advantages to students who must complete their terminal writing requirements and get on with the business of their lives. There are several powerful advantages of such research. Among the most immediate and apparent of those advantages is (1) ability to capture contextual effects; (2) broader-based data-gathering; and (3) greater power to capture the human dimension (Soltis 1990, 248). For example, with qualitative research it is possible to understand subtle things not usually revealed in quantitative research. Examples of such subtle understandings are, why certain children thrive in certain learning contexts; the child-rearing and valuing practices of

Mexican-American families as related to education; and language "code-switching" behaviors of successful African-American professionals.

You can complete many qualitative studies quickly, without the time-consuming wait for data required in certain quantitative studies. However, the actual amount of time required usually is a matter of your commitment, informed backgroundanddiligence.

Be sure you have adequate access to research contexts. Completion of certain studies requires reasonable access to appropriate research contexts. Let's return to the first example given in Chapter 1, *A Validated Curriculum Alignment Procedure for Elementary Curricula.* A student without access to a school district could not possibly complete such a related thesis, dissertation or project! Before you adopt a research design or complete a research proposal, you must evaluate the actual "do-ability" of that research. Without reasonable, frequent access to the appropriate context, the research cannot be completed.

Do your best to secure the support and advocacy of your faculty committee. You experience significant advantages when one or several faculty members are actively interested in your thesis or dissertation topic. This means that your thought process during adoption of a topic should include assessment of potential faculty interest in your topic. Remember that the ability to enlist the support of faculty members bears directly on your speed of completion of terminal scholarly activities. Chapter 5, *The Commonsense of Choosing Terminal Scholarly Committees,* covers this point in some depth.

More than 20 models for writing and developing (organizational patterns) terminal scholarly activities are available to individual students who have a general idea about their research interests but are unable to get started with "Dreaming Creatively" about their theses, dissertations or projects.

The companion book to this one, entitled *21 Models for Developing and Writing Theses, Dissertations and Projects,* can serve all students who are ready to write theses, dissertations or projects. For students who have managed to generate well-articulated, precise and clearly delimited topics, this book provides *more than* 21 ways to organize and develop those topics. The "organizational patterns" are basic thesis or dissertation types (models) that you can combine and vary, depending on topics involving non-experimental research. The book is equally effective for those of you who have one or several ideas that must be "harnessed,"and organized as theses, dissertations or projects. The options presented in the book are ways of "plugging in" and developing those ideas.

The book can also help students with "dreaming creatively" about their theses, dissertations or projects. The term "dreaming creatively" was first used in one of my *Research Methods* classes by a female student whose name escapes me. Since then, I have used the term repeatedly because it captures the essence of the process, and because each person involved in the process must somehow move beyond what is known in quest of the unknown, toward new knowledge.

Much of the remainder of this chapter is about "dreaming creatively." However, before going to that subject, it is important to dispel one or two popular notions. The first is that every thesis, dissertation or project topic must be something that is so radically new that it holds the promise of revolutionizing an entire field of endeavor. On the contrary, terminal scholarly activities usually result in small additions to the knowledge base of a field. The second notion is that developing a worthwhile, original topic for a thesis, dissertation or project requires creative genius or some kind of divine inspiration. Nothing could be further from the truth; almost all students who are well-read in their fields and interested in their real-world workplaces can generate worthwhile, original topics.

What is meant by "Dreaming Creatively?" Dreaming Creatively is the process of developing your thesis, dissertation or project idea so that you can move smoothly into writing and completing your study. Before "Dreaming Creatively," you should

1. Be sure you understand clearly the goal of terminal scholarly writing requirements.
2. Be sincerely interested in at least one major problem area in your field.
3. Develop one or more "hunches" about causes of problems and related possible solutions.
4. Read extensively about various aspects of the problem(s) as well as solutions proposed by other writers and experts.
5. Solicit the opinions of persons who work in and are affected by the problem area.

You should understand each requirement before moving ahead. First of all, throughout the process of "Dreaming

Creatively," you should bear in mind your objective. That overall objective is identification and selection of a topic that is (a) an original, meaningful contribution to the literature of the field, (b) interesting and acceptable to professors of a committee of faculty members, and (c) feasible and "do-able" within a reasonable time span.

Second, when you are conscientious about solutions to problems encountered in your field, you are more likely to persist in activities that lead to those solutions. For example, workers in fish and wildlife management should care about the impact of introduction of fish or animals from foreign environments; teachers of bilingual students should wonder about the variables that stimulate success for some children, so that those variables could possibly be applied to other children; nurses working in lower socioeconomic neighborhoods should be interested in better ways of communicating about proper prenatal health care with pregnant women in those areas; and transportation managers of school districts should be interested in the relative cost and efficiency aspects of diesel and gasoline buses for serving their districts. Your interest is the major element of your basis for genesis of theses, dissertations and projects. Without it, your attempts to generate topics often meet with failure; or worse still, they result in shallow, irrelevant topics.

There is one more powerful argument for sincere interest on your part. In the middle stages of development of terminal scholarly documents, it often is the case that distractions or even simple boredom interrupts your continuity, leading to lengthy time periods when you do little or no work. For most persons, sincere interest in their topics will *compel* consistent, regular work on their theses, dissertations or projects!

The "hunches" referred to in (3) are important because they often are the bases of topics for studies, and equally important, one or several hypotheses that form the basis for the investigation that follows. A natural consequence of the sincere interest discussed in (2) above is one or more "hunches" about the reasons things, good or bad, are operating in some worthwhile endeavor. It often is the case that persons confronted with problems for which they sincerely desire solutions often develop "gut feelings" or "hunches" about possible causes and potential solutions to those problems. This is especially true when they actually work in the context of those problems----so that potential solutions also offer the promise of improving their worklives.

After you have developed several informal "hunches" about causes and possible solutions, the next logical step (4) is for you to develop an informed background on problems and solutions in your area of interest. For example, suppose a teacher of predominately Portuguese bilingual students wants to stimulate lagging parent interest and participation in the school activities of students. Before attempting to improve that parental participation, the teacher should learn as much as possible about the cultural values, child-rearing practices and other related aspects of Portuguese-American parents. That search for improvement might lead to a dream topic, *A Procedural Model for Improvement of Involvement and Participation in School Activities by Portuguese-American Parents.* This would qualify as a thesis because of the promise of generalizable findings about improvement reflected in the model. You should note that two of the best sources of information about such problem areas are existent theses and dissertations, most of which conclude with a section called *Recommendations for Further Study.* If you have not yet chosen a topic, you might find several viable suggestions for topics in these sections of relatively recent theses and dissertations.

Finally, you should (5) solicit the opinions of persons who work in the problem area. Often, persons who are on the cutting edge of daily practice will suggest other, previously untouched areas of importance. Frequently, students have ideas that could help with overcoming problems in certain fields, but they are unsure about whether those ideas are important enough. Before committing themselves to theses, dissertations or projects targeted at such problems, they must develop confidence that the research is worthwhile. In such situations, the best resort is to "pick the brains" of persons who work in contexts affected by the perceived problems.

"Dreaming creatively" about a thesis, dissertation or project. Development of a title is the first and most important step in writing theses, dissertations or projects. Appropriately selected and properly written, the title becomes a directional compass for beginning and completing the document. Let's take a look at what a well-written title accomplishes. A title

1. Determines the direction of the research.
2. Provides the boundaries within which the research must occur.
3. Excludes content not relevant to the research.

An example is best for helping you to grasp the essentials of developing a title. Development of a title was one of the most important requirements of my research methods class. The great majority of students wisely approached the task with the intention of developing topics that they could use later for their theses. I am proud to say that virtually all of my students had approvable titles at the end of the semester.

So that students were able to get started early in the semester, I always explained the basic elements of theses, dissertations (and projects) during the first week of class, with emphasis on the all-important requirement of generalizability. Then I asked them to visualize titles on their theses as though they were complete and bound, with gold lettering on navy backgrounds. The assignment was three possible titles for each student, based on problems and possible solutions wherever they work.

During the second class meeting, in a graduate class atmosphere of free expression of ideas, students slowly revealed their tentative titles. As discussion ensued with one student idea, other students busily revised their own tentative titles as they observed my discussion of ways of arriving at logical, "do-able" topics.

I can recall two students whose experiences in topic development will be instructive here. The first one was an experienced teacher interested in the school performance of foster children. She was the first to volunteer to expose her proposed title to the scrutiny of others. As she read the title aloud, I wrote it on the board:

Why is it that children from certain kinds of foster homes and certain kinds of family makeup patterns seem to do better in elementary reading as measured by the Comprehensive Tests of Basic Skills (CTBS)?

Although she posed it as a question, the essential element, *the quest for generalizability*, was there. Woven into her question-title was interest in findings applicable to other settings. The terms "certain kinds of foster homes" and "certain kinds of family patterns" suggested a strong interest in generalizability.

First of all, I showed the class that the scope and breadth of her proposed study were well beyond that required for a Master's thesis. As the title stood, it included both boys and girls in *all* elementary grades. Furthermore, it was not necessary to specify the standardized test in the title. Other class members were busily revising their own proposed topics as I spoke.

Class members began to volunteer suggested rewrites of her topic. One was

Why 5th grade girls from certain foster homes perform better on Standardized Achievement Tests in reading

One class member asked whether gender differences were important. She said no. Following that exchange, another title offered was

An analysis of the relationship between certain foster home variables and 5th grade Reading Achievement

I explained the distinction between *co-occurrence* and *causality*. It was possible to find co-occurrence of certain foster home variables and reading achievement fairly easily, in existent records. However, it would be virtually impossible to show the existence of cause-effect relationships between certain foster home variables and achievement.

A week later, after hearing my lecture on the major types of research, she finalized her topic,

Reading Achievement of 5th Graders as Related to Identified
Foster Home Variables: A Causal-Comparative Study

After she gained the critically important conceptual *Gestalt* (overall feeling of getting an important, do-able topic), the rest was easy. Within months, she

1. Performed an exhaustive ERIC (Educational Resources Information Center) search through the college reference librarian, with emphasis on foster homes, foster home placements, courts and foster children, school achievement of foster children, and many other related subtopics.

2. Wrote chapters 1, 2 and 3.

3. Explained her study, promised confidentiality, and secured permission from three school districts to gain access the cumulative files of foster home students.

4. Searched "backward" (over a 10-year span) through the school records of more than 700 students and former students who had been foster home children, focused on the extent of co-occurrence between certain foster home attributes (one parent, two-parent, older siblings, no older siblings, income levels, etc.).

5. Developed quantifiable independent variables that subsequently were correlated with reading achievement, using the *Contingency Method of Correlation.*

6. Wrote chapters 4 and 5----finis!

The second example is even more illustrative. One of the most interesting cases of "dreaming creatively," in the same *Research Methods* class, was that of a School Administration major interested in the status of school building bond elections throughout California. She presented her title:

Are there patterns of income, age and family configurations that explain why bond issues pass in some districts and fail in others?

Another question, but I concluded long ago that the "hunches" necessary to get things started actually start as questions in the minds of those in the throes of "dreaming creatively." Before discussion of that title could get underway, she offered another title in the same interest area:

Why is that school building bond issues fail in some really affluent communities in California and pass in other less affluent ones where debt service is much more difficult?

She explained that while writing a related paper for a school finance class on the subject of school building problems in California, she noticed that elections for bonded indebtedness passed in some districts and failed in others, but no demographic reasons or influences could be found. Variables like average ages of adults, socioeconomic levels of districts, average ages of school board members, length of service of superintendents, ratio of young families to older families, all failed to reveal reasons why bonding elections passed in some school districts and failed in others.

Then I challenged the entire class: why worry about situations where bond issues *fail?* After all, the real interest was in where, and more important, *why* they *passed!*

The class picked up on the point immediately. One class member said, "Why not identify the school districts that passed bonding elections and then find out what is common to them?" I should add here that, as always, teachers at all levels enjoy seeing the productive spontaneity they have encouraged in their classes, and I was no exception.

I challenged them again: where was the generalizability? What general findings could be extended to other situations and school districts?

Then, the student who posed the topic spoke again, offering yet another version of her topic:

An Experience-Based Model for Passing a School Bonding Election in California

She explained that she would like to look, both qualitatively and quantitatively, at a large number of "successful" school districts in the interest of finding out what was common to them, and then put together a "step-by-step model" (her expression) that presented a procedure based on those common qualities. After all, she knew already that the State Department of Education had identified the successful districts.

This led to my brief discussion of the differences between theoretical, conceptual and procedural models. Following that, she went to the board and changed her topic by inserting three more words, *procedural, School* and *Districts:*

An Experience-Based Procedural Model for Passing a School Bonding Election in California School Districts

In a few months, her thesis was complete. Methodically, she

1. Called the State Department of Education and asked for information identifying those school districts that had been successful in bonding elections.

2. Performed an exhaustive national literature survey that included, among other things, variables that typically are identified with successful bonding elections.

3. Using information gleaned from the literature on survey research, prepared, pilot-tested and sent a questionnaire to school superintendents or their designees in the "successful" school districts. She also asked for any available information about the bonding election and the preparatory events leading up to it.

4. After receiving and analyzing mounds of data from various school districts, she identified the elements most common to all of the "successful" districts.

5. Developed and presented a *procedural* model based on those common elements, complete with timelines, persons involved, inservice requirements, community meetings, media relations and other critically important elements. (Chapter 4 is the proper place for models, following *Analysis of Findings*).

6. Completed Chapter 5 and finalized her thesis!

Five Steps in "Dreaming Creatively" The "steps" listed below actually are loose guidelines that are likely to work for most of you. They seemed to work for most of my students.

1. *Write several versions of a topic that seems to "capture" all aspects of a problem that needs a solution in your field.* At this point, think only of the problem and your "hunches" about causes and solutions and be sure to avoid the common tendency to choose only research ideas that conform to research methods you prefer. At this point, you should feel free to entertain thoughts that might even seem outlandish and well beyond the realm of possibility. You should think freely, as long as your thoughts are directed to meaningful problems and possible solutions that promise generalizability.

2. *Evaluate the breadth of the topic. Too much? Not enough?* You should remember the dangers of overambitiousness discussed in the first chapter. Remember that terminal scholarly studies rarely result in "be-all-end-all" outcomes. Instead, these studies "inch along with the knowledge base," contributing small additions to knowledge in a field.

   The first question that you should ask is, "Is the topic ambitious enough?" If the answer is yes, continue on to the next question, "Is the topic too ambitious?" If the second answer is yes, the task ahead is one of narrowing the breadth and scope of each topic. For example, a master's thesis that originally was entitled, *A Statewide Assessment of Evaluation Practices in City Management* might be narrowed to

An Assessment of Evaluation Practices in Five Selected California Cities.

Or a dissertation that originally was entitled

The Application of Stepwise Multiple Regression to Analysis of Input-Output Relationships in 20 Urban Budgets

might be changed to

Decision-Making: Stepwise Multiple Regression as a Validated Optimization Tool in City Budgeting.

In both cases, changes in titles changed the scope and breadth of the studies. In the first case, the Master's study, the change is obvious. The change in the second case is subtler; whereas the first study involved 20 applications of the statistical procedure, the second study involved only four or five. Also, the derived generalization, the ultimate hope of all scholarly studies, would be much more obvious.

You should note a subtler, very important point in the second dissertation title. The second title suggests the introduction of a model----in this case, an "optimization tool." Students who can visualize and somehow derive validated operational models are well on their way to successful completion of theses and dissertations.

A Master's candidate might change from a proposed thesis entitled,

Resource Identification: A Model for Use in Development of a Community-Based Resource Directory of Services for Persons with Mental Retardation

to a *project* entitled,

A Three-County Resource Directory of Services for Persons with Mental Retardation.

3. *Assess the data availability as well as your access to research contexts.* Your basic question here is a simple one: "Now that I have the dream, can I get at the data in order to actualize it?" This is an ever-present problem for all persons involved with scholarly research, and a "yes" answer must be possible before moving ahead with plans.

4. *Delimit the topic to the fullest extent possible without losing its compelling interest.* "Delimitation" excludes topics that your study will not cover. It is critically important for defining the boundaries of the study. It occurs in three places. The first is in the topic itself; that is, reduction in the breadth and scope of topics occurs during topic development. The second is in the proposal submitted to members of Master's or dissertation committees; and the third is in the first chapter of the thesis or dissertation. Usually, effective faculty committee members will insist on delimitation, because they know that neither theses nor dissertations can cover *everything.*

However, it is important to note that there are restrictions on delimitation. You cannot exclude topics that are logical expectations of informed readers in a subject area, unless you give adequate justification for the exclusion. Another way of saying this is that you cannot arbitrarily exclude topics because they are inconvenient or require too much time and energy for adequatecoverage.

Your title can help to delimit your study in many important ways. Limitations on aspects such as timespan, age groups, gender, socioeconomic status, problem categories, years of experience of participants and many others inserted into your title all help with delimitation.

---

5. *Assess the feasibility of completion of each topic.* Is it possible to enlist a supportive faculty committee for the topic? Are there other barriers to completion? Even after developing a great topic and finding an available research context, you can still run head-on into legalities and politics that can interfere with or even make research impossible. For example, there are legalities against disclosure of personal information, and most agencies will want assurances that you will maintain confidentiality. There are also legalities related to bargained rights of employees.

For example, teacher organizations defend their teachers against classroom invasions. It is easy to imagine teacher organization objections to certain types of research that require the participation of teachers.

Ethical restraints represent another barrier. There are ethical considerations applicable to both human and non-human subjects. Students should be sure that they understand those ethical "limits" before they finalize plans for their theses, dissertations, or projects.

Cost is one more feasibility consideration. Certain research projects involve costs, for computers, computer programs, test copies, scoring services, mailing, experimental devices, feed for laboratory animals, storage costs, traveling and others----not to mention the costs of personal upkeep and "survival" until studies are completed. Students should be sure that they can meet all costs until completion.

Two Sample "Organizational patterns" for Creative Stimulation. The two sample "organizational patterns" presented below are limited extracts from the companion book to this one, entitled *21 Models for Writing and Completing Theses, Dissertations or Projects.* That book presents each organizational pattern together with a general description, examples, and a recommended procedure for development. You should think of "Organizational patterns" as templates or models for writing terminal scholarly studies. In most cases, persons with hunches and basic ideas about *what* they want to study are likely to find one or more ways related to *how* to develop those ideas.

The two organizational patterns are presented here in skeletal form for two reasons. The first is illustrating how easy it is to conceptualize and develop a thesis topic, especially if a framework or "organizational pattern" is available. The second reason is getting you interested in the content of that book full of thesis ideas.

The Broad-Based Assessment. This model for developing and writing (organizational pattern) or avenue to beginning and completing a thesis is the easiest of all. Assessments are applicable to virtually any activity imaginable. Examples are without limit: business must periodically conduct needs assessments of their employees; foundations must conduct assessments of the effectiveness of the contributions they make to various causes; police departments are forced to periodically assess equipment effectiveness; unions must frequently assess the understandings, needs, and outlooks of members related to factual aspects; and it is frequently necessary to conduct periodic assessments of the state of the art in various fields.

Generalizability, the result of effective questionnaire design, sampling, and survey procedures, leads to field-applicable findings. These findings often suggest new strategies for overcoming various field problems.

The literature of a given field is likely to reflect current theory along with certain practical aspects. However, contact with practitioners is the only way that you evaluate the "cutting edge" of daily practice in that field. Broad-based assessments can yield such information, accurately and with relatively little effort.

Students should understand the following main points about Broad-Based Assessments:

1. Broad-based assessments can readily evaluate field needs, skill levels and needs, knowledge bases, or program modification needs and other related operational aspects in fields of concern. The overall intent is establishment of baselines related to areas of concern, in the interest of revealing areas needing improvement.

2. Interest areas of broad-based assessments are derived from problems that need solutions within a field.

3. Choice of interest areas of broad-based assessments require vigorous defense, based on problems that need solutions in a field.

4. Questionnaires, interviews or telephone surveys are prime avenues for completing Broad-based assessments.

5. Properly designed instruments, with Likert scaled response formats, lend themselves to statistical analysis. Such analyses carry considerable appeal with individuals in the professiorate who favor quantifiability in virtually all studies.

6. The intuitively pleasing character of Broad-based assessments "sells" quickly with many faculty members.

It is important to answer two related questions here. The first is "How can a broad-based assessment constitute an entire 'organizational pattern?' " And the second is, "How does broad-based assessment yield useful generalizability, a central interest of all theses and dissertations?"

The breadth and scope of the assessments provide answers to both questions. When and if a well-planned, well-designed assessment is broad enough to encompass an entire population of respondents, its revealed outcomes can frequently afford accurate generalizations about that population. The long-range hoped-for outcome, of course, is provision of a starting point for improvement of practice in areas of concern.

The need to know dictates the nature, scope and breadth of assessments. Felt needs and inadequacies perceived by clients, practitioners, or consumers of organization services stimulate Broad-Based Assessments.

Broad-based assessments require, first of all, an *informed* background in your field. Frequently, the recurrences of several problems in an agency or institution indicate the need for and importance of an assessment. Interviews of fairly small numbers of persons intimately familiar with daily field problems represent one way of determining whether a problem is a significant one. Evaluation of the number and nature of customer complaints in stores, the number and recurrence of grievances in bargained settings, or summative evaluations of effectiveness in various agencies and businesses are other indicators.

There is also the matter of the actual importance of a given problem. There is no need for needs assessment unless evidently something, some inadequacy, inconsistency or recurrent problem bothers virtually all practitioners in an interest area.

The nature of the endeavor dictates the type of assessment needed. For example, corporations frequently require management training needs assessments; health agencies require community health needs assessments; cities need housing needs assessments, and the list goes on and on.

Various sources of information lead to or suggest initiation of assessments. Questionnaires sent to clients related to other operational aspects might lead to the decision that a needs assessment is in order. Several legal claims or possible lawsuits might suggest the importance of an assessment; or clear indications of service inadequacies might point to the necessity to find out what is or is not working.

Let's take a look at the wide range of needs assessment interests found in just a handful of topics:

Continuing education needs of midwives who serve Arizona Native-Americans

Support Needs of Re-Entry Students in Higher Education

Evaluation of the Cultural Awareness and Sensitivity of Production Line Managers who Supervise Hispanic Bilingual Workers

A Statewide Assessment of School Administrator Knowledge of Bilingual-Bicultural Education Principles

A Survey of Needs Related to Job Satisfaction of Music Educators inCalifornia Urban Secondary Schools

Perceived Needs of Teachers who Work w/SMR Students

Almost any field needs an accurate profile of its dominant practices!

The Profile of Dominant Practices. In many if not most fields, the literature related to current effective practices lags well behind actual changes in practices. In many cases, this time lag occurs over several years. This happens for several reasons. One is the extent of demographic change in various areas of the nation. Another is the variations in rates of adoption of technological changes in practices in businesses and agencies in different areas and jurisdictions. A third, frequently related to the first two, results from legislative mandates in various states.

Such a lag is a major concern of both university and government researchers in various areas. Obtaining a *Profile of Effective Practices* is often an efficient, economical approach to gaining a picture of what is happening on the cutting edge of daily practice. When you obtain such a profile in ways that permit generalizations, you enhance the literature of the field.

Here are several main points that characterize *Profiles of EffectivePractices* :

1. Profiles of dominant practices are aimed at assessing current operational state of the art in fields of concern, with emphasis on dominant practices and priority of importance of available approaches to practice. The overall intent is to inform other practitioners in the interest of improvement of their practices within the field.

2. Interest areas on which profiles of dominant practices are based are derived from questions, controversial and otherwise, that need answers within a field. They require vigorous defense, based on important unanswered questions in a field.

3. Sources of information related to profiles of dominant practices are surveys, questionnaires, opinionnaires and personal interviews.

4. Like Broad-based assessments, Profiles of dominant practices represent another intuitively pleasing organizational pattern.

5. Profiles of dominant practices lend themselves to statistical analysis, provided you set yours up in Likert-type scaled response formats.

This "organizational pattern" is almost as easy as the Broad-Based Assessment. One added challenge it presents is the requirement that researchers possess *detailed* familiarity with practices in the field of interest.

You should think of a Profile of Dominant Practices as an "information switchboard" for practice, because it offers several aspects that can afford generalizable findings that are important to practitioners. The first aspect is revelation of variety in field approaches to practice, including combinations of approaches. The second is the extent of co-occurrence between practices and measured output. The third aspect is the resultant hierarchy of relative effectiveness, measured in output or production terms; and the fourth is clarification of the advantages and disadvantages of various methods and combinations thereof.

Some examples, illustrated with fictitious studies, are:

An Achievement Hierarchy of Methods Used in the
Regulation of Nonpoint Source Pollution

The Relative Accuracy of Five Approaches to Forecasting
Slaughter Cow Prices in Five Western States

Three Effective Culture-Specific Approaches to Improvement
in
Use of Public Health Care Services by
Oregon Hmong Populations

Four Experience-Based Methods of Extending the Shelf Life
of Roasted and Ground Coffee

Summary

"Common sense" must be a dominant theme when students consider topics for their theses, dissertations, or projects. That commonsense theme, which incorporates three important dimensions, must always temper the idealism that often guides and drives research.

1. Topics selected for theses, dissertations or projects must be those that can be accomplished within the timelines of the personal lives of students.

2. Students should select only those topics for which they have assurances of access to appropriate research contexts.

3. Topics selected for terminal scholarly activities must be those for which faculty support is available. Ability to enlist the support of faculty committees is critically important to successful completion of their terminal scholarly activities.

"Dreaming creatively" about a thesis, dissertation or project refers to the first and most important step in writing theses, dissertations or projects----development of a title. Appropriately selected and properly written, the title becomes a directional compass for beginning and completing the document, because it:

1. Determines the direction of the research.

2. Provides the boundaries within which the research must occur.

3. Excludes content not relevant to the research.

Fortunately, "dreaming creatively"can be taught, provided student researchers (1) arm themselves with well-informed backgrounds about problems of interest; and (2) are interested in one   or several field problems that need solutions. "Dreaming creatively" is taught and encouraged throughout this book as well as its companion volume, *21 Organizational patterns for Beginning and Completing Theses, Dissertations or Projects.*

4

A SIMPLE, SAFE TWO-PART "FORMULA" FOR AN EFFECTIVE SCHOLARLY WRITING STYLE

Even after years of English, Literature and other classes that demand or should demand quality writing, many students still produce poorly written papers. Unfortunately, most teachers never gave these students definite procedures for doing so.

This chapter presents a successful, easy-to-follow "formula" that you can carry into and through your terminal scholarly research activities. As you read and practice this formula, remember that no instructor anywhere can offer generalities that apply to *all* thesis, dissertation or project formats. Such generalities are impossible, since most college departments will detail their preferred style manuals and conventions.

You must be able to write *within the meaning* of captions in the basic format of the thesis, dissertation or project proposal presented to your committee.

While it would seem that the standard captions found in publication style manuals for theses, dissertations and projects are self-explanatory, students nevertheless tend to confuse the content of certain captions. Since these errors occur in proposals as well as theses, dissertations and projects, we need to discuss them separately.

Before moving on, we must make an important distinction between two *basic frameworks*, one for thesis or dissertation proposals and another for actual theses or dissertations. Although there are significant variations from institution to institution, one generally accepted *basic framework for proposals* is

Precise Title
Introduction and Background of the Study
Statement of the Problem to be Researched
Significance of the Study
Delimitations
Definitions of Terms
Method and Procedure of the Study.

And a *basic framework for theses or dissertations* is

Chapter I - <u>**Introduction and Background of the Study**</u>
   Statement of the Problem
   Significance of the study
   Statement of the hypothesis(es)
   Operational Definitions
   Assumptions and Limitations
   Delimitations of the Study

Chapter II - <u>**Review of the Related Literature**</u>

Chapter III - <u>**Methodology and Procedure**</u>
   Setting of the Study
     Population and Sample
     Design of the Study
       Null Hypotheses (if appropriate)
       Criterion/Alpha levels
       Statistical Method
       Instrumentation
       Data collection procedures
       Data analysis

Chapter IV - <u>Analysis of Findings</u>

Chapter V - <u>Summary, Conclusions, Implications and Recommendations for Further Study</u>

We will refer to the two frameworks throughout the remainder of this chapter. Please maintain your awareness of the distinction between proposals and actual theses.

Errors in writing to proposal captions. Students typically make three errors when they write proposals. The first occurs in the *Introduction and Background*, where students actually combine the content of *Statement of the Problem* and *Importance of the Study*. This creates a problem because the basic proposal format provides for each. Strangely, this confusion occurs while these students neglect the critically important thorough scene-setting required in the *Introduction and Background* section. A second error results when students confuse *Statement of the Problem* and *Significance of the Study,* two captions with distinctly different interests. Third, students write improperly within the meaning of the *Delimitations* caption, frequently including aspects that are not delimitations. You should focus on writing precisely within the meaning of each caption, explained below.

Precise Title. You should make sure that you have a precise title that is thoroughly delimited *before* submitting your proposal to your committee members. If you are in doubt, discuss your indecision with your committee chairperson. Then and only then should you write your proposal.

Let's base all examples that follow in this section on the (fictional) precise title,

*A Qualitative Examination of the Motivating Influences of
High-Achieving College Bound African-American
High School Graduates*

Introduction and Background of the Study. This section usually is a brief sketch giving background information necessary for reader understanding of the proposal. It is intended to "reel in" each professor-reader as a possible committee member. It is most effective when it is (1) focused *only* on the background of the problem to be presented later, (2) succinct and to-the-point, and (3) supported with enough documentation that clearly illustrates the need for the proposed study.

> *When you cite a data base search in your proposal, you calm Committee fears about duplicating existent research. Always include the date, search descriptors and synonyms used, and the number of articles found.*

When writing this first section, you should remember that your intended readers are *uninvolved* (the term "naive" is often used here, and I believe that it is improper). An uninvolved reader----in this case, a professor----might be quite knowledgeable about the overall field of interest, but uninformed about the specific topic. This means that it is important to be thorough, with reasonably detailed scene-setting and a thorough information backdrop.

Although committee members refuse to talk about length, redundant, lengthy proposals irritate them. Remember that these professionals devote much of their time to reading student papers and other thesesand dissertations. This means that you should make your proposal as short and to-the-point as possible without losing any essential elements.

A brief example of the way to approach this section, based on the topic in the preceding paragraph, is

Introduction and Background of the Study

One of the most perplexing, persistent problems facing American education is the underachievement of African-American students of lower socioeconomic backgrounds. That such underachievement appears to be associated in no small measure with socioeconomic background is no surprise. However, since education is very closely related to vertical mobility in virtually all occupations in American society (source year, page), the problem is extremely troubling. Without improvement in school performance, many if not most African-American children are likely to continue to be non-competitive in salary marketplaces.

Many scholars have studied this problem. A mid-1996 ERIC search conducted by this writer revealed more than 2100 titles published on the subject between 1985 and 1996. Still, meaningful solutions are not forthcoming at this time.

One problem characteristic of virtually all of these studies is focus on the negative behaviors, skills deficits, parental shortcomings and other aspects related to students who fail (source year, page; source year, page; and source year, page). It is possible that much more fruitful research would result from intensive study of the defining, pervasive characteristics and motivating influences of African-American students of lower socioeconomic backgrounds who have managed to succeed in spite of the negatives of the environments in which they find themselves.

There is precedent for this approach. Both bodies of research, *School Effectiveness* (source year, page) and *Teaching Effectiveness* research (source year, page) large-scale examples. Focusing *only* on "more effective schools" and "more effective teachers," respectively, as defined at the outset of the investigations, these studies yielded findings that resulted in dramatic changes in the practices of running schools and teaching, respectively.

Statement of the Problem to be Researched. This is a specific statement of what the research intends to accomplish. Here, too, students should go directly to the central message of the section:

Statement of the Problem

The central problem to be researched in the proposed study is identification of salient motivating influences characteristic of college-bound high-achieving African-American high school graduates of low socioeconomic backgrounds. These influences are likely to include parental values and influences, peer influences, significant others and many other unknown variables.

Significance of the Study. This is essentially an explanation as to why the proposed research is important, and why it is a potential contribution to the field. You should remember that the central interest of this section is "selling" the study to a committee. Its emphasis should be on why the study is worthwhile.

Significance of the Study

This proposed study is significant because of its potential contribution to the literature focused on one of the most difficult problems facing American society. In addition to its potential for shedding light on those <u>successful</u> behaviors common to high-achieving African-American students, the study will examine several approaches to <u>qualitative inquiry</u> that could be useful to future researchers in this broad content area

Delimitations. This section is for excluding certain aspects not considered in your study. The process is exactly one of "walling out" those aspects that are beyond the scope and purposes of the study. Much has been written throughout this book about differences between theses and dissertations, and one notable difference is in the extent of delimitations, with the former more severely delimited.

How does one choose delimitations? The answer is that informed readers in a given subject area will hold certain basic expectations for it. In the present example, it is likely that informed readers will wonder (1) about the criteria for determining achievement levels at the outset of the investigation; (2) what sources will be used to determine the salient qualities of the students; (3) whether gender differences are important; (4) how "significant others" are defined, and several other aspects.

Although the *Delimitations* section will tell these informed readers *what not to* expect, you should be aware that this section cannot be used arbitrarily, excluding those aspects that are somehow difficult to research, or narrowing the breadth of the study to the convenience of the researcher. To the contrary; you should never use the Delimitations section to arbitrarily exclude aspects that are the normal expectations of informed readers.

Delimitations

In the proposed study, African-American students who attended non-public schools will be excluded. Excluded also will be African-American students whose family incomes exceed those of families that are defined by the California State Department of Education as "lower socioeconomic." Selection of study participants will be based solely on grade point averages earned between 10th and 12th grades, inclusive.

Gender differences are excluded as relevant considerations in the proposed study. "Significant others" as applied in the study will be limited to parents by birth or marriage, older or younger siblings, relatives, church influences and in-school adults like teachers, counselors, coaches and others. Finally, salient motivating influences as revealed in the study will be limited to those influences that are plausibly related to school success, as determined by the researcher.

Definitions of Terms. Here, you must remember that proposals as well as actual theses, dissertations or projects must be "pitched" to uninvolved readers, those persons who might be generally knowledgeable about the overall field, but not the specific topic. For this reason, certain terms unique to the specific topic might not be within the operating vocabularies of all readers.

This means that definitions of terms are frequently necessary. What terms should you define? The answer is simple: only those that are (1) outside of or new to the "jargon" or typical usages of the field; and (2) those coined by the writer because of lack of adequate existent definitions.

Whenever possible, sources should accompany definitions used. Whenever no sources exist, the researcher should so state and coin a new term, accompanied by the clear statement that it is an author coinage.

Definition of Terms

The terms defined below are offered in the interest of clarity. Some, derived from the literature, are so documented. Others were coined by the investigator for purposes of interpretation within the context of the present study.

Educational Criticism. This is a method developed by Eisner (1979) which utilizes a combination of methodologies: those of art critics and ethnographers in combination, applied to analysis of salient characteristics of educational contexts. Relying on an informed backdrop and well-developed ability to look, see and appreciate (called *Educational Connoisseurship*) the educational critic uses *Sturctural Corroboration* and *Referential Adequacy* in reliability, validity, and other matters of inference.

Flat talk. A term frequently used by African-Americans of lower socioeconomic groups to characterize language with poor enunciation.

Method and Procedure.   Like the *Significance of the Problem* section, this section also "sells" the proposal to would-be committee members. You should avoid vagueness here; the best "sell job" of all occurs when you list, in sequence, your *specific* proposed steps for accomplishing the study.

Remember that you should explain your methodology precisely, so that someone else could conduct the same study under identical conditions.

Method and Procedure of the Study

Accomplishment of the proposed study will adhere to the following steps.   It is possible that some may occur simultaneously. Those steps are:

1. An exhaustive survey of the literature germane to Chapter 1 (*Introduction and Background of the Study*), Chapter 2 (*Review of the Related Literature*) and Chapter 3 (*Method and Procedure*).

2.   Securing permission from the Oakland, San Francisco and Los Angeles school districts for access to files of graduates in high schools selected on the basis of high numbers of African-American students of lower socioeconomic backgrounds.

In each case, the necessary assurances of anonymity and confidentiality will be given.

3. Simultaneous development of questionnaires to be given to identified students themselves and significant others when appropriate.

4. Analysis of data found in files, by (a) identifying study subjects using minimal grade-point criteria in college-bound coursework; and (b) searching "backward" through cumulative folders of each identified student for logical causal factors and common "threads" among the graduates.

5. Mailing questionnaires to appropriate "significant others" of students for whom addresses are available.

6. Conducting telephone interviews of students for whom phone numbers are available.

7. Development of qualitative analysis of findings, to be reported in Chapter 4.

8. Development of summaries, conclusions, and recommendations, presented in Chapter 5.

Other captions sometimes required in proposals. As has been stated repeatedly throughout this book, college and university departments will differ significantly with respect to their specific requirements. You can modify the proposal format presented above to include several other aspects. Some of these are:

Specific Objectives of the Proposal. This refers to an explicitly stated, detailed account of the expected outcomes of the proposed research.

Assumptions. These are suppositions that one or more aspects are true without further proof or discussion. Assumptions can be facts, statements, axioms, postulates or notions that require no further clarification.

Hypotheses. Hypotheses are tentative statements about relationships between two or more constructs. They are statements of specific relationships that grow out of the "hunches" that stimulate studies and investigations. There are many kinds of hypotheses, and many faculty members believe that they are critically important for keeping student researchers "on track." Null hypotheses developed in Chapter 3 (Method and Procedure) result from the initial conceptual hypotheses developed in Chapter 1. These null hypotheses dictate the framework for application of statistical analyses.

Proposed Generalizability. Generalizability refers to the usefulness and applicability of research outcomes to other similar settings. Many consider it the ultimate aim of research, and some faculty members wish to see explicit statements about where the results of research are likely to be applicable.

You can *quickly* learn a safe, simple two-part "formula" for a scholarly writing style equally applicable to proposals, theses, dissertations and projects.

Part I: Adherence to six simple conventions will dramatically improve both the mechanics and quality of your writing.

Convention I: Generally, you should write *proposals* in the future tense. ("The investigator will demonstrate;" or, "It is the intention of the proposed research to draw a discernible relationship between..." or "it is expected that the proposed research will demonstrate the effectiveness of...") By contrast, you should write actual theses, dissertations and projects in the *past* tense. ("One of the conceptual hypotheses that led to the study was that the research...")

Convention II: Write proposals as well as their related theses, dissertations and projects in third person: ("the investigator," *not* "I").

Convention III: You should write proposals and their related theses, dissertations and projects in the plural when possible and appropriate. ("children," *not* "the child; " "teachers," *not* "the teacher.")
More than any other single convention offered in this section, use of plural will enhance the scholarly tone and language of terminal scholarly documents, because it eliminates the need for the awkward-but-common "his or her" usage that has no place in scholarly writing.

Convention IV: Write proposals as well as theses, dissertations and projects with no contractions. In combination with Conventions II and III above, this convention will immediately help to enhance the scholarly style of students. Try it, you will like it!

Convention V: Write proposals, theses, dissertations or projects using language and tone addressed to an audience of peers----Master's degree and beyond. It is also important to remember to write terminal scholarly documents in the language of the field. You should practice, simulating the language of other scholarly documents.

The "formula" offered in this section will help the language and tone aspects of terminal scholarly activities. One more tip is appropriate: you should visualize your intended audience as you select words, phrases and other usages in scholarly documents.

Convention VI: Proposals should include reasonable source documentation, a point often overlooked by students who tend to think of documentation as necessary only for actual theses, dissertations and projects. Documentation of sources in proposals serves two important purposes.

The first and most important aspect of adequate documentation is that it is evidence of adequate scholarship prior to adoption of a topic, an admirable quality in a student. It also creates the impression that it is not likely that the topic is a direct duplication of existent research, that you have performed the necessary searches that avoid such duplication of effort.

General.   Generally, you should write theses, dissertations or projects exactly like proposals, except for tense. You must remember to change from the *future tense* of your proposal to the *past tense* of your thesis, dissertation or project.

Part II: Adhering to a "patterned writing" approach offers an effective solution for students who have problems writing scholarly documents.

Learning and adhering to a "patterned writing" approach offers an effective solution for students who have problems writing scholarly documents. Chapters 1, 3, 4 and 5 present few if any problems for those adhering to a "patterned writing" approach.

However, Chapter 2, *Review of the Related Literature*, presents a special challenge that you can overcome observing a few cautions. Chapter 2 is frequently challenging because of abundance of literature in certain fields and the resultant necessity for making judgments about selection and exclusion of literature. Adherence to a "patterned writing" approach helps you to organize appropriate content in Chapter 2. Organization of Chapter 2 is discussed in Chapter 6.

"Patterned writing" helps you to keep your terminal scholarly ventures organized from start to finish. It applies to quality scholarly papers (term papers) as well as theses, dissertations, and projects. For many of you familiar with instructional approaches used in the military, "patterned writing" follows the old maxim, "Tell 'em what you're gonna tell 'em, tell 'em, then tell 'em what you told 'em. Let's illustrate it with an excerpt from a fictitious thesis topic. A portion of Chapter 2 of that fictitious thesis, entitled *Beyond the Glass Ceiling: Patterns of Vertical Mobility Among Women Executives in Banking*, provides the basis of the example.

CHAPTER 2

Review of the Related Literature

Because of the relative recency of nationwide concern about the vertical aspirations and mobility of women, there is now an abundance of related literature on and tangential to the topic. This means that the coverage of aspects of that literature pertinent to this investigation must be limited.

Thus, adequate review of the literature pertinent to the current investigation necessitates coverage of the following broad topics: (1)   A Brief History of Women and Occupations in America Since the Suffrage Movement; (2)   The Effect of the Women's Movement on Occupational Mobility; (3)   General Trends in Occupational Change and Vertical Mobility for Women: Some Statistics; (4) The Current Status of the "Glass Ceiling;" (5)   Characteristics of Effective Opinionnaires as Survey Instruments.   Discussion throughout the remainder of this chapter adheres to that sequence.

A Brief History of Women and Occupations in America

Since the

Women's Suffrage Movement

Since the Women's Suffrage Movement in the early decades of this Century, both the occupational aspirations and opportunities for women have changed dramatically.   It is the purpose of this broad section to examine certain pivotal changes since that period, together with concurrent events in American history that seemed to accompany or parallel them.

Further, it seems appropriate to explore this brief history on the basis of significant eras in the history of our country since then. The eras chosen as relevant are: (1) World War I and the Postwar Recovery Period; (2) The Great Depression; (3) World War II and the Postwar Recovery Period; (4) The Korean War and the Postwar Recovery Period;   (5) The Launch of the Russian "Sputnik" and the Decade-Long Reaction of America; (6) The Effect of Movements of the 1960s on the Women's

Movement; and (7) Vertical Mobility for Women in the Current Conservative Political Era.

World War I and the Postwar Recovery Period

The Great Depression

World War II and the Postwar Recovery Period

The Korean War and the Postwar Recovery Period

The Launch of the Russian "Sputnik" and the Decade-Long Reaction of America

The Effect of Movements of the 1960s on the Women's Movement

Vertical Mobility for Women in the Current Conservative Political Era

Here, you should return to the next centered heading identified in the opening statement of the chapter:

The Effect of the Women's Movement on Occupational Mobility

After thorough development of this section, go to the next centered heading in the opening statement of the chapter:

General Trends in Occupational Change and Vertical Mobility for Women: Some Statistics

You should write with freedom here on the basis of what is revealed in the literature. Then, continue with the next centered heading. Got it?

Notice the inclusion of a centered heading section related to the instrument used in the study:

<u>Characteristics of Effective Opinionnaires as Survey</u>
<u>Instruments</u>

Choice of this topic and placement here, in *the Review of the Related Literature*, is optional. It could have been placed in Chapter 3, *Method and Procedure*, under a caption called <u>Instrumentation</u> or <u>The Instrument</u>. However, whenever the the researcher designs the questionnaire, it is a good idea to clearly explain the design criteria for questionnaires, together with sources in Chapter 2. This amounts to a defense of the questionnaire design chosen. Actual questionnaires, should be placed in the Appendix, in the exact order in which discussion of the questionnaire occurs in the narrative.

Now let's apply the same "patterned writing" approach to a "skeletal" format for Chapter 3, *Method and Procedure.* Note that it follows the same logic as the sequence offered above.

CHAPTER 3

Method and Procedure

As discussed in Chapter 2, the general method of this study necessitated a comprehensive survey sent to a randomly selected group of women executives in the banking business in California. This chapter describes the general procedure employed in the present study. Discussion ensues under the following broad headings: (1) Setting of the Study, (2) Population and Sample, (3) Development of the Questionnaire, and (4) Statistics Used to Interpret Findings.

<u>Setting of the Study</u>

<u>Population and Sample</u>

<u>Development of the Questionnaire</u>

<u>Method Used to Interpret Findings</u>

Students typically experience problems with the organization of their literature reviews. Most problems are organizational because of the abundance of literature in most fields; that is, decisions must be made as to what literature to include and exclude.

However, the "patterned writing" discussed here is just as applicable in Chapters 1, 4 and 5. Researchers who adhere to it can quickly present well-organized, well-written theses, dissertations or projects to their committees for final approval!

Style manuals are important as guides to orderly presentation and documentation of scholarly writing. Students should learn the conventions in style manuals typical of their fields and adhere to them in development of their theses, dissertations, or projects.

For most theses or projects, you should adhere to one of three style formats, depending on the preferences of faculties of your department:

1. Campbell/Ballou Form and Style in Thesis Writing.
2. Publication Manual of the American Psychological Association
3. Turabian's A Manual for Writers of Theses and Dissertations (Based on the *Chicago Manual of Style*).

Detailed references are offered in the Bibliography. Each format has its advantages and its traditions. For example, the empirical sciences like Chemistry, Physics, Biology and others usually adhere to the Campbell/Ballou form. Its great advantage is quick reference to sources which are located on the bottom of the page. The APA Publication Manual usually is the standard in Counseling, Psychology and related disciplines. Compared to the Campbell/Ballou approach, it is an easier, quicker method.

Adherence to the *Chicago Manual of Style* is easiest of all. It is the *de facto* publishing industry standard for most publications, especially books. In the absence of a departmental preferences, you should explore and use this approach, which requires (only) author name, year and page number in parenthesis following each statement or quote. You can present references in simple alphabetical order at the end of the entire document. You can easily learn this method by investigating most published books.

Certain departments sometimes prefer other more specialized style manuals. You will find several listed at the end of this chapter.

Often, students mistakenly believe that style manuals afford instruction in English composition or grammar. To the contrary, these style manuals assume competence in these areas. This means that students who need help along these lines should consult books written for those purposes.

Adhering to comprehensive checklists prior to submitting proposals or finalizing theses can save time and effort during terminal scholarly activities.

Before you submit proposals and actual thesis, dissertation or project drafts, you should attempt to eliminate every possible non-substantive error or problem. This argues for a checklist that covers most aspects of documents submitted.

It is probably helpful to remind you that research proposals have two major interrelated purposes. The first is guidance and development of your thesis, dissertation or project; and the second is securing the consent and support of a Committee of professors in the development of those activities.

It is virtually impossible to offer a "generic" *sample* proposal that covers every type of proposal possible. To understand that point, imagine the great differences between *qualitative* and *quantitative* proposals.

Proposals. The major points listed below should be part of one or more checklists that you should review before submitting *proposals* to your committee.

I. The *Title* should name the study population, and be as succinct as possible, including major variables studied, implicit or explicit relationships between major variables.

II. The *Cover sheet* should adhere strictly to department requirements.

III. The *Introduction and Background of the Problem* should (a) adhere to an approved style manual, (b) have subheadings at appropriate levels, (c) contain citations for references, (d) explain the personal interest that led to the study, and (e) contain a brief history of the origins of the problem.

IV. The *Statement of the Problem* should (a) make a direct, succinct statement of the problem studied, (b) list the hypotheses, (c) list assumptions and (d) clearly explain the intended generalizability of the study.

V. The *Importance of the Study* section should explain (a) the contribution of the study to the knowledge base of the field; (b) importance of the study to practitioners; (c) the relationship of the study to current theory and to a few important related studies; and (d) the basis or logic for presentation of the problem.

VI. The *Definition of Terms* should (a) include only terms unique to the study, or those not in general usage in your field; (b) cite a source for each definition used; or (c) clearly state that the term is your coinage, used in the absence of an appropriate term.

VII. The *Delimitations* section should (a) "fence in" your study by making appropriate explicit statements about what it *does not* cover; and (b) make sure that only delimitations are included in the section.

VIII. The *Method or Procedure* section should explain (a) the setting of the proposed study; (b) the research design; (c) the population and sample; and (d) detailed step-by-step procedures for accomplishing the study.

IX. The *Bibliography* should be based on a format that is consistent with the style manual adhered to in the body.

Theses, dissertations and projects. For actual *theses, dissertations* or *proposals* many of the conventions listed above will apply. Several more are listed below.

I. The *Title* should be the same one on the approved proposal.

II. The *Front Matter* should adhere to department requirements, which generally include a (a) title page, (b) approval sheet, (c) table of contents, (d) list of tables, and (e) list of figures.

III. *Chapter One* should include (a) a thorough problem background, (b) an explicit statement of the problem, (c) a statement of the hypotheses, (d) a thorough description of the significance of the study, (e) operational definitions, (f) clearly stated delimitations, (g) assumptions and rationales, and (h) limitations, which include restrictions on generalizations and conclusions.

IV. *Chapter Two* should (a) present a detailed history of the problem; (b) review related literature; (c) address important polemics and views related to the topic; (d) review literature related to the methodology when not commonly understood or employed in practice; and (e) offer a succinct summary.

V. *Chapter Three* should generally present methodology with the detail necessary for possible replication. It should (a) describe the setting of the study; (b) explain the research design; (c) explain the treatment, including procedures and techniques of data collection, statistical procedures, and (d) explain the method and bases for conclusions in qualitative studies.

VI. *Chapter Four* should (a) introduce and explain the manner of presentation of results; (b) present findings; (c) discuss findings in light of the hypotheses adopted; (d) avoid conclusions; and (e) in projects, include a complete copy of the product.

VII. *Chapter Five* should (a) summarize the study; (b) present conclusions in light of the original questions that stimulated the study; (c) present implications for practice within your field; and (d) offer recommendations for further study.

VIII. The *Bibliography* should (a) adhere to a format consistent with the style chosen; and (b) include a citation for each reference as well as others for recommended reading.

IX. The *Appendix* should (a) explicitly illustrate points made in the text; (b) generally, include all items that would otherwise interrupt narrative continuity if placed in the text; and (c) have items grouped categorically and arranged *in order of occurrence in the text.*

Summary

For both proposals and actual theses, dissertations or projects, you should begin by adhering to a basic framework or outline. College or university departments usually suggest or require basic frameworks.

Write *within the meaning of* captions found within the basic framework. When writing their *proposals,* students make three errors (1) erroneous inclusion of *Statement of the Problem* and *Significance of the Problem* in the *Introduction and Background* development; (2) confusion of *Statement of the Problem* and *Significance of the Study;* and (3) writing improperly within the meaning of the *Delimitations* caption.

You can *quickly* learn to use the safe, simple two-part "formula" for a scholarly writing style presented in this Chapter. Combine this "formula" with the conventions in the style manual typical of your field and adhere to both during development of your terminal scholarly document.

TIP BOX 1: A CALENDAR FOR FINALIZING YOUR THESIS OR DISSERTATION TOPIC

You should begin to develop thesis or dissertation ideas and topics while taking required coursework, no later than the first day you enroll in *Research Methods.* Before you are eligible for formal faculty advisement, you can develop original topics. Follow the sequence below and you will avoid many problems along the way.

While taking coursework

1. Keeping a file of all term papers and lecture notes of all of your courses taken will remind you of previous research sources as well as the beliefs, preferences, biases and idiosyncrasies of various professors. This knowledge will help (a) when you formulate your faculty advisory committee and (b) during required oral examinations.

2. Unless instructed otherwise, write all term papers in the style manual format required by your department. Write your thoroughly documented term papers in the five-part format characteristic of scholarly papers: (1) *Introduction and Background,* (2) *Literature Review,* (3) *Methodology,* (4) *Findings,* and (5) *Summary, Conclusions and Recommendations.*

TIP BOX 1 (Continued)

3. Start by looking for possible topics in your interest area in *Master's Abstracts* and *Dissertation Abstracts,* two sources present in all college and university libraries. Read *Recommendations for Further Research* and *Implications for Practice,* (in Chapter 5) in theses and dissertations written in your department as well as others written elsewhere. Develop a file of recommendations you find in completed studies and group them by content area and date.

5. Write as many titles as you can think of that "capture" your interest. Study them frequently, then select and rank the top five.

6. Ask your university reference librarian for a synonym-based computer search of a data bank of your field. The idea is to *rule out the possibility of duplicating existent research.*

7. On the basis of your interest, choose three of the five titles, and write a *two-page* proposal on each. *Be sure to include a statement about the computerized data search, including the date.*

8. Ask your *Research Methods* instructor for a critique of each proposal.

9. Choose two of the three titles, based on your interest and the reaction of your instructor.

10. Develop the two proposals. Include a complete bibliography.

11. Take the two proposals to a faculty member of your choice. That professor should be someone (a) in whose classes you have done well and (b) interested in your content area. If possible, choose a senior, Full Professor----for reasons explained throughout this book.

12. If you receive a positive written reaction from the faculty member of your choice, schedule an appointment soon thereafter. During the appointment, ask that faculty member to serve as chairperson of your thesis or dissertation committee.

5

THE COMMONSENSE OF CHOOSING COMMITTEES

Like many humans elsewhere, many faculty members are self-serving and, to an extent, ego-involved in their endeavors. These faculty department members experience serious conflicts due to professional opinions, jealousies, faculty politics, and simple interpersonal differences. These aspects carry strong implications for students who are trying to complete their theses, dissertations and projects.

Students whose proposed research is compatible with the professional preferences of one or more professors are likely to get advocates for their theses or dissertations. The same is true when a student research interest is a meaningful subset of research currently underway by one or more professors. Such advocacy can often clear the way to smooth, quick completion of terminal scholarly research.

This suggests that there are several practical, common sense aspects to choosing M.A. or doctoral advisement committees, called terminal scholarly committees throughout this book. This brief chapter explores several of these practical dimensions.

A strong caveat about this Chapter.   One point made throughout this book is that many college and university faculty members are self-serving and ego-involved, frequently at the expense of student interests. It is important to clarify that observation in the interest of helping readers to temper and keep in perspective the remainder of this chapter.

You should understand that the college or university workplace represents a distinctive culture, with its own guiding values, competing factions, frictions, rewards, disincentives, and most importantly, political dynamics. Within this unique workplace, there are various faculty members of different ability levels, energy levels, backgrounds, and interests. While there are differences from faculty to faculty, it is probably safe to say that faculties are more alike than different.

Let's return to the main point. Many faculty members are self-serving in the sense that they may be working on one or more larger research projects that could be enhanced considerably as a result of research surfaced by their students. Although this might appear unethical or even ruthless to the observer unfamiliar with the climates of university workplaces, it is not unusual. Many foremost, well-known scholars regularly glean ideas, findings, and even directions for new research from the modest efforts of their Master's or doctoral students!

Many if not most faculty members are also ego-involved in their scholarly opinions.   As suggested above, this condition is basically human and it is reinforced by the reality that many faculty members have committed themselves to a lifetime of scholarly research based on their scholarly opinions.

You should take these generalizations offered about faculties "with a grain of salt."   That is to say that the observations made about dealing with faculties and their members are cautions and points to observe.

Finally, in fairness to all of my colleagues, most want little more than quality work by good students. It is also safe to say that most came to the professorship because of such sincere interest.

> *Understand faculty rank and power and you can avoid being caught in political "crossfires" between faculty members*

You enjoy several advantages when you take the time to understand the rank, tenured status and related aspects of faculty members whom you wish to enlist as chairpersons and committee members.

The best characterization of the closely related terms "professor" and "professional" is autonomy in the work sphere. That is to say that persons who are "professional" have no "bosses" lurking over their shoulders. Within limits, they operate on their own, guided by their professional values and ethics.

The autonomy in the work sphere mentioned above means that no one invades the classrooms of professors and attempts to dictate what or how they teach. College professors and their organizations zealously guard this professional privacy, commonly known as "academic freedom." Even college administrations must tiptoe carefully around the "turf" staked out by professors, who often refer to themselves collectively as "the community of scholars."

This "community of scholars" defines its "turf" as the curriculum----what is taught and how it is taught. Professors and their organizations protect that turf in two ways. The first is tenure, the lifelong guarantee of employment; and the second is collective faculty action, through faculty senates and collective bargaining where permitted by law.

Tenured professors are relatively powerful. When they also are "full" (formally designated "Professor") rather than associate or assistant professors, they are extremely powerful in the context of the university.

For these reasons, when you are able to enlist the support of a full professor as a chairperson you enjoy clear advantages. One is the ability to overcome bureaucratic hurdles. Another is a strong spokesperson who can "sell" your proposed topic and their basic ideas to other professors or committee members.

You should understand the basic professional opinions, values and biases of the professor you wish to enlist as chairperson of your Master's or doctoral committee.

Every thesis, dissertation or project reflects professional opinions, intentional or not, implicit or explicit. Consider the problems faced by a student who has generated a proposal laden with ideas, assumptions and theories that are in conflict with those of a professor who could otherwise be an excellent, powerful chairperson. It is not likely that a student would be able to enlist that professor as a chairperson.

> *Before asking a faculty member to serve as your Committee chairperson, review old lecture notes, syllabi, course outlines and other course material presented by that faculty member. You should be sure that you understand the viewpoints, biases and preferences of that faculty member.*

Many if not most faculties reveal strong biases toward quantitative research with experimental designs. At least half of my students experienced initial rejection of their thesis or dissertation proposals when those proposals did not involve statistical testing. Clearly, most faculty members favor quantitative research designs.

Unfortunately, students frequently are *coerced* into experimental research designs, for three reasons. First, experimental approaches seem "safer" because they appear to be more scientific and closely related to the methods of empirical sciences. Second, since many faculty members were also "coerced" into quantifiable research approaches during their own Master's or doctoral studies, they are more familiar with the hypothesis testing paradigm involving null hypotheses and various statistical tests. Third, the dominant research paradigms throughout the 20th Century have been largely quantitative, adhering closely to the methods of the empirical sciences----a trend characteristic of emerging fields attempting to establish respectable identities.

All of this means that when students prefer non-experimental research, they frequently run into opposition by professors. The same is true of qualitative research. Some researchers report that this resistance has diminished recently (Eisner and Peshkin 1990, 3-7). Still, non-experimental research often presents alternatives that are much more viable for many students whose budgets and timeframes are limited.

You should seek as chairperson professors in whose classes you made very high grades.

Senior professors consent to chair your Committee because they believe you can deliver a thesis, dissertation or project with a minimum of correction, editing and general oversight. For this reason, you should first of all seek as chairperson a professor in whose classes you made very high grades, especially on term papers.

You should also be familiar with that professor as an instructor. You have performed well on examinations, term papers and other aspects, it is likely that you will be thoroughly familiar with the professional opinions, biases, preferences, communications style and expectations of that professor.

You should retain all old class notes from each instructor in your M.A. or doctoral courses. The ability to recall certain professional opinions, biases, preferences and other aspects of each instructor is extremely helpful when enlisting their support.   That ability is equally helpful during oral examinations following successful completion of theses, dissertations and projects.

This means that in such situations, the confidence and understanding should be mutual. What better way to start the arduous task of completing a thesis, dissertation or project?

You should enlist the support of the Chairperson before talking to other would-be committee members. This might be the most important of all of the cautions offered in this chapter. Successful, early completion of your terminal scholarly activity relies heavily on the advisement, leadership, and advocacy of your chairperson.

One of the worst mistakes made by many students is attempting to enlist the support and participation of several faculty members on their committees independently, without understanding the relationships and interpersonal dynamics between those faculty members. Often, the result is a committee of persons whose conflicts due to professional opinions, jealousies, faculty politics, and simple interpersonal relationships are such that successful completion of terminal scholarly activities are difficult if not impossible. In such situations, students are often caught in "crossfires!"

The best commonsense alternative, then, is for each student to attempt to *enlist the chairperson first*. Then, ask that chairperson to suggest the names of other faculty members. The result is likely to be a compatible, smooth functioning committee that offers the best possibility of quick completion of a thesis, dissertation or project.

Present to the Chairperson a well-written draft of the thesis or dissertation proposal at the first meeting. There are several reasons for having a well-written draft of a thesis or dissertation proposal ready in the first meeting with the potential chairperson. Such a well-written, well-developed proposal helps the student to demonstrate (1) reasonable knowledge on the topic; (2) originality of the topic; and (3) *definitiveness*, something that can be "pinned down" to specifics. Often, the potential chairperson will indicate acceptance by signing in the appropriate place then and there, followed by a suggestion that the student-candidate submit copies of the proposal to two or more other *specific* faculty members to round out the committee!

The important point here is that students are miles ahead when they can show a potential chairperson that: (1) they have one or more specific topics in mind; and (2) that they have done enough "data snooping" to insure that their topic or topics represent original research. Such "data snooping" is easy; any college or university reference librarian can provide computer printouts of similar studies surfaced through synonym-selected searches.

One last point is important. While students should have only one well-written formal proposal on hand, it is a good idea to have other topics and ideas, in writing, in the unlikely event the one selected does not interest the potential chairperson.

Summary

You should understand that the college or university workplace represents a distinct culture. Within that culture exists a unique set of guiding values, competing factions, frictions, rewards, disincentives, and political dynamics. Within the college or university workplace, there are various faculty members of different ability levels, energy levels, backgrounds, and interests. While there are differences from faculty to faculty, it's probably safe to say that faculties are more alike than different.

You should take care to understand the faculty rank of persons you wish to enlist as chairpersons and members of your thesis, dissertation or project committee. It is important to remember that rank and status on college or university faculties mean power that can translate into strong advocacy that means early, successful completion of theses, dissertations and projects.

It is also important to understand clearly the professional opinions, biases and attitudes of potential chairpersons. Doing so is likely to ensure that your proposed ideas and topics are compatible with the views of potential chairpersons.

For completion of your terminal scholarly activities as quickly as possible you should:

1. Attempt to enlist as chairperson a faculty member in whose classes you made very high grades.

2. Always attempt to enlist the support of the chairperson first, well before talking to other potential committee members.

3. Always have a well-written proposal ready at the first meeting with the potential chairperson. It's also a good idea to bring along a list of alternate topics.

TIP BOX 2: SOME INSIGHTS ABOUT DEVELOPING AND CONDUCTING SURVEYS

I. Questionnaires must be *convenient* and *efficient.* They should consistently elicit accurate information with a high percentage of returns.

II. Questionnaire items should match the language levels of respondents.

The following items are sample items aimed at high school students:

    1. Your grade level is ___10th   ___11th   ___12th

    2. Considering your height, are you happy with your present weight?

    I am   ___much too light ___too light ___just about right
        ___a little too heavy ___much too heavy

    3. Required dressing for all P.E. classes is

    ___important ___unnecessary ___embarrassing sometimes

By contrast a questionnaire pitched to *principals* might be:

    1. How would you characterize your administrative "style" with respect to supervisory evaluations of teachers?

    ___clinical supervision ___administrative monitoring
    ___peer supervision   ___eclectic (a combination of all)

    2. How many times in the past three years have you written negative documentation of the performance of a teacher, to the extent that remediation and supervisory oversight were required?   ___Once ___2-3 ___4-6 ___7-10 ___None

TIP BOX 2 (Continued)

III.   Another vitally important consideration in the development of questionnaires is time required to respond to them accurately and thoroughly. Questionnaire formats must emphasize time economy. The remaining sample questions, aimed at busy teachers, represent several distinctly different formats available to students who are devising questionnaires.

  1. In which of the following age groups do you belong?

         ____22-29____30-39 ____40-49 ____50-59 ____60 or over

2. In the event of a procedural or other bargaining contract violation by your principal, how likely are you to initiate a grievance?

____Definitely grieve   ____Probably   ____Undecided____Probably not____Definitely not

IV. Directions should be clear and aimed at definite, unambiguous responses.

DIRECTIONS: Please record your response on a rating scale of 1-9. Encircle the number that best represents your opinion.

How do you rate the new basal reader, *Broad Horizons* in terms of

  2. Its matchup with your district Language Arts framework?

     1 2 3 4 5 6 7 8 9
     poor   very good

V. For time economy, clarity and statistical analysis, the Likert response mode is best.

DIRECTIONS: Encircle the response that best represents your opinion.
SA=Strongly agree, A=Agree, N=No opinion, D=Disagree, SD=Strongly disagree

1. Your principal is qualified to evaluate teaching of high school chemisty.

     SA   A   N   D   SD

2. Current bargained evaluation procedures violate my academic freedom.

     SA   A   N   D   SD

Always provide a *Comments* section at the end of questionnaires.

6

WRITING THE FIRST THREE CHAPTERS

As discussed repeatedly throughout this book, once a topic is selected, delimited and outlined, the remainder of the work involved in completing theses, dissertations or projects is relatively easy. In most cases, subsequent development will take care of itself, especially if you adhere to the points and tips offered in the first four chapters of this book. This chapter is about how to write the first three chapters.

Many committee members like to see a first draft of your first three chapters as soon as possible. Other committees encourage data gathering while you write the first three chapters. At any rate, you should write and submit the first three chapters together when possible, because they set the stage for the remaining two chapters.

Most students run into problems when writing Chapter 2. This happens for two reasons. The first is that no formula or pattern exists for organizing Chapter 2. The second reason is that you must make many decisions about what literature to include and exclude, *without* a guide or formula. For these reasons, you should pay close attention to the section in this chapter entitled, *About the organization of Chapter 2 of your study.*

Illustrated in this chapter are extracts from two fictitious terminal scholarly papers. The first, a quantitative approach, is simplest. The second, a qualitative approach, presents a greater challenge because of greater variety in both "ways of knowing" and possibilities related to content and organization.

At this point, you should make a serious attempt at starting your own writing. Try the ideas and sample language within these pages, in the context of your own interest.

Whether quantitative or qualitative, theses or dissertations use the same general pattern of organization or *basic framework for theses or dissertations*:

Whether quantitative or qualitative, theses and dissertations follow the same general organizational pattern. Throughout this chapter, that organizational pattern will be called the *basic framework for theses or dissertations* . The chapter sequence of that organizational pattern is Introduction and Background; Review of the Related Literature; Method and Procedure; Analysis of Findings; and Summary, Conclusions and Recommendation.

Notice the second, qualitative study presented in this chapter. The meanings of the chapter titles, captions and sub-captions remain the same, even though the names are different. Note that in that study the typical Chapter I caption, *Introduction and Background* , was changed to *The Nature of the Study* ; and Chapter V, *Summary, Conclusions and Recommendations*, was changed to *Quality of Instruction: Exploring the Elusive.* This is permissible, as it amounts to an important exercise of your individual creative latitude, as long as you keep the essential content of each chapter consistent with the original five-part outline.

Remember these points if and when you attempt to write a "skeletal" version of your first three chapters:

1. Be sure to write precisely within the meaning of each caption.
2. As you write, refer to the "Six Conventions" of Part I of the "two-part formula."
3. Be sure to adhere to "Patterned Writing," Part II of the "two-part formula."

For many theses or dissertations with *quantitative* emphases, actual writing and completion is largely a matter of adherence to captions adhere to the *basic framework for theses or dissertations*

It is best to start with the *basic framework for theses or dissertations,* a general outline for organizing the first three chapters of your thesis or dissertation. These outlines vary somewhat from one style manual to another. Graduate student handbooks distributed by graduate schools frequently offer variations preferred by those schools. One version of the *basic framework for theses or dissertations*, introduced in Chapter 4, is reproduced below:

Chapter I - Introduction and Background of the Study
    Statement of the Problem
    Significance of the study
    Statement of the hypothesis(es)
    Operational Definitions
    Assumptions and Limitations
    Delimitations of the Study

Chapter II - Review of the Related Literature

Chapter III - Methodology and Procedure
  Setting of the Study
  Population and Sample
  Design of the Study
    Null Hypotheses (if appropriate)
    Criterion/Alpha levels
    Statistical Method
    Instrumentation
    Data collection procedures
    Data analysis

Chapter IV - Analysis of Findings

Chapter V - Summary, Conclusions, Implications and Recommendations for Further Study

It is best to think of this as a "starter" framework. This means that certain captions will not apply in some cases; and in others, you will have to add certain captions.

We can illustrate use of this outline with a fictitious thesis entitled, *A Statewide Assessment of School Principals' Knowledge of Attention Deficits Disorders (A.D.D.) and Related School Problems.* Not only is this an emerging issue in the schools; revelations of administrator strengths and weaknesses in this area could afford generalizations that could in turn lead to needed training programs or even legislative action.

We can start by looking at a sample introduction in Chapter 1:

CHAPTER 1
Introduction and Background

Recent advances in medical technology, coupled with a

plethora of new findings in brain research, have ushered in a new wave of possibilities in educational improvements. In the last five years, brain research has presented the powerful possibility that almost 29 percent of behavioral and learning problems in the schools are attributable to attention deficits disorders (A.D.D.) (_____1994, 11). Very little imagination is necessary to see that many of these same behavioral and learning problems extend to adult criminal behavior and the challenges of rehabilitation and reduction of prison recidivism. What is most exciting is the reality that virtually all of the problems lend themselves to early adjustments through medication, coupled with counseling and pro-active parental and teacher behaviors (Ibid, 14).

Like all new findings which impact schools, these must somehow permeate the consciousness of all educators, teachers, administrators, teacher aides and others. Achieving such broad, widespread awareness in individual schools is the proper province of the school principal who exercises several critically important controls in schools. Among these controls are the authority to (1) exert administrative control, (2) exert aggressive instructional leadership, (3) control the evaluative framework of the school, (4) control the distribution of rewards, and (5) control the flow of information and resources in the school (Webster 1994, 5).

This means that the thorough dissemination of information related to A.D.D. is essentially in the hands of principals, and...

We will continue this with a fictitious *Statement of the Problem:*

Statement of the Problem

_____and _____ (1987) contend that supervisors----principals----as well as teachers share the responsibility of improving instruction in classrooms. The general literature of supervision reflects the position that knowledge of principles of teaching effectiveness is an absolute "must" for all supervisors, especially principals.

At this time, little research exists relative to the most effective role of school administrators in developing and ensuring quality teaching approaches to the problems of children with attention deficits disorders (A.D.D.). A valid argument is that in-depth knowledge on the part of principals must precede meaningful improvements in such teaching approaches.

Thus, the problem researched in the present study centered on discerning and establishing a baseline knowledge profile of

California school principals relative to the problems of children

with A.D.D. Specifically, the study was aimed at providing

answers to several questions:

1. What is the extent of knowledge or conceptual grasp of California elementary site administrators (principals) relative to attention deficits disorders and related problems in their schools?

2. To what extent are elementary principals prepared to effectively evaluate teachers in the context of their handling of problems incidental to A.D.D. in classrooms?

3. What aspects of academic and professional backgrounds of respondents appear associated with enhanced knowledge and awareness of the techniques and dynamics of providing quality education to students with attention deficits disorders?

4. What are the needs for further professional development for administrators in this area?

Many students have problems writing within the *Significance of the Problem* section in their theses, dissertations or projects. For some reason, they write more than necessary, while straying far from the central interest of the section. One or two simple statements can satisfy the general requirement of this caption:

Significance of the Problem

The current study derived its significance from its potential

for shedding light on several important aspects of the emerging

area of research on the impact of Attention Deficits Disorders

(A.D.D.) on American education. The present study addressed

specific voids in the knowledge base related to A.D.D. One was

essentially an evaluation of the state of the basic competence of school principals in understanding and evaluating the effectiveness of programs and teaching aimed at A.D.D. students; and equally important, the second was an assessment of the critically important future professional development needs of these principals.

Similarly, the *Delimitations* section is also confusing to many students. This section presents an opportunity for writers to exclude many aspects that would otherwise be ordinary expectations of informed readers. Here's a good approach to this section in the context of this same study:

Delimitations of the Study

This study was restricted in scope to assessment of the knowledge and attitudinal competencies of those California school administrators whose span of control included responsibility for the education of students with A.D.D. Neither program effectiveness nor analysis of specific approaches to A.D.D. interventions were central concerns of the study. Finally, gender differences among students, teachers, or administrators were not considerations related to the outcomes of the study.

You should use the *Delimitations* section carefully and conservatively. The following are delimitations typical of many research studies:

1. Exclusions related to gender differences.
2. Exclusions related to socioeconomic backgrounds.

3. Absence of concern for the size of cities, organizations, utility districts or school districts studied.

4. Exclusions related to years' training or experience.

About the organization of Chapter 2 of your study. Because of the abundance of literature in most content areas, organization of Chapter 2, *Review of the Related Literature,* presents one of the most challenging tasks for most students. That is to say that you must eventually make decisions about what literature will be included and excluded. While it is difficult to generalize about the organization of Chapter 2, a few points might be helpful:

1. You should select literature for inclusion in Chapter 2 with the *uninvolved reader* in mind. This means that your coverage of background or introductory material "paint a picture" with enough detail for the uninvolved reader.

2. It is a good idea to start Chapter 2 with a historical account of the issue or problem central to the thesis or dissertation. You should refer to that point in Chapter 4 in the discussion of "patterned writing."

3. Remember to include literature related to controversial points, dichotomies, arguments or major differences between theorists on a topic, with balanced representation of both viewpoints.

4. You must support and defend any concept, construct or instrument that you conceptualize or devise for use in the research. The literature review presents an

excellent opportunity for such a defense. For example, if you devise, say, an opinionnaire for assessing the attitudes of Hmong parents toward western medicine, you must defend it. You can defend it in several ways. One is by citing *the non-existence* of such an instrument in the literature. A second is citation of literature related to other effective attitude assessments of that population. Third, you can cite general principles of effective questionnaire and survey design on which you based your questionnaire design.

Chapter 4 discussed the format and content of your thesis or dissertation in the context of a study entitled *Beyond the Glass Ceiling: Patterns of Vertical Mobility Among Women Executives in Banking.* Return to that section before you attempt to write Chapter 2 of your study.

The format and organization of Chapter 3 of Theses and Dissertations. In a nutshell, the aim of Chapter 3 is clarification of the research procedures of the study. A condensed version of Chapter 3, (*Method and Procedure*) based on our current example, might be quite instructive here:

CHAPTER 3
Method and Procedure of the Study

The aims of this study were identification of (1) the

supervisory knowledge bases of elementary and high school

principals relative to the problems of children with A.D.D.; (2)

selected relevant information regarding the academic and

experiential backgrounds of principals; and (3) demographic data of their schools. This chapter describes the methodology toward those ends.

In order to address these issues, the chapter was divided into three broad sections. The method of data collection was described, followed by a description of...

Data Collection

A survey and cover letter (Appendices A and B) were developed for purposes of collecting the following information:

1. The knowledge bases of principals relative to effective instruction of...

2. The opinions of principals relative to characteristics of effective programs for effective diagnosis, treatment and remediation...

The *California Public Schools* Directory, which contains a complete listing of all public schools in California was obtained. The relative proportions of elementary, middle, and high schools were calculated in the interest of insuring proportional representativeness in the sample used in...

Instrumentation

A three-part survey (Appendix B, pp. 74-75) was developed for the study. The survey consisted of 40 items, divided into three sections. The first 25 items were in the format of a Likert-type opinionnaire. Topics of the opinionnaire were based on knowledge of instructional methodology, with particular emphasis on...

Statistical Analysis

A scoring method was adopted in the interest of establishing the relative levels of knowledgeability and administrator grasp of...

The Opinionnaire

The first section of the survey consisted of a 24-item Likert-type scale (____1967) designed to assess the previously-discussed areas. Fifteen of the items described ideal instructional and program characteristics. The remaining nine items described...

Items were carefully worded to avoid specialized terminology which might not be familiar to respondents. After all, the objective was not to...

Inferences for the Survey Data

The dependability of the survey results for formulating conclusions about characteristics of the population was a major concern both before and...

Two distinctly different methods for making inferences were tried, with only slightly different results. The first approach, following a method suggested by _____(1987, 42)...

Response Mode

Five response categories were provided for each item: *strongly agree, agree, unsure, disagree, and strongly disagree.* Administrators were asked to read each...

Scoring

Each response category was assigned a value ranging from 5 to 1 with a response of *strongly agree* given a value of 5; and *strongly disagree* given a value of 1,...

Administrator and Site Backgrounds

The second section of the survey consisted of nine questions pertaining to... While the existence of causal relationships was not the focus of the study, the extent of co-occurrences could be determined between...

Open-ended Questions

Three open-ended questions were provided in the third section of the survey, pertaining to student needs, program features, and programmatic needs and goals. Purposes of this section included determination of the following:

1. Do principals place the pressure for low graduation rates on the students, or do they perceive that the educational programs are inadequate for student needs?

2. Do effective program features result from...

3. Are the future goals of principals for A.D.D. programs consistent with current research findings?

Automation of Statistical Analysis Procedures

A spreadsheet was designed using *Lotus 1.2.3* (Lotus Development Corporation 1991) in order to summarize scores for each item, and also to compare...

You must present Chapter 3 so precisely that someone else could conduct your study if necessary. Chapter 3 must identify and describe the population and sample, as well as the study context. It must also describe procedures and techniques, including instruments used and statistics applied.

Starting with the *basic framework for theses or dissertations* will do much to ensure effective organization and elimination of duplicated or non-essential content.

Chapter 2 of this book underscored the importance of *Understanding the possibilities in qualitative research methods*. You should re-read that section and explore the possibilities of qualitative research before finalizing your thesis or dissertation topic.

There exist no generalized outlines of studies with *qualitative* emphases, because each topic dictates the content of captions. Closer inspection shows qualitative studies adhere to the same overall chapter-by-chapter sequence as quantitative studies. Let's try another example that might help to portray an approach to a qualitative study.

The outline below shows the unfoldment of a *qualitative* approach to a dissertation. You should compare its logical progression to that of the outline of the quantitative one offered earlier. Although no pattern is available for writing qualitative studies, note that each caption selected helps to enhance the broader section under discussion. It is based on an *actual* topic entitled, *Don't Be Teachin' Jovita Wrong: An Exploration of Reading Instruction in Four Urban Third Grade Classrooms*. The author kindly granted permission for use and exposition of this topic.

Chapter I - The Nature of the Study
   Introduction
      Assessments of Compensatory Education: 1965-78
      New Directions: Practical Inquiry in Study of Classrooms
      Problems with Theory
      The Need for Practical Inquiry
      Using Educational Criticism for Practical Inquiy
      Some Limitations of the Study
      Organization of the Dissertation

Chapter II - <u>Review of the Related Research</u>
    Effective Teaching in Primary Grades
    Reading Instruction in the Primary Grades
       How should reading be taught in primary grades?
          Affective aspects of reading instruction
    Issues in the Education of Low-Income Black Children
    Conflicting orientations toward the children
         Language differences and reading
         Emerging Issues

Chapter III - <u>Design and Procedures of the Study</u>
    The Setting of the Study
       The cumulative deficit in achievement
       The large decline at end of third grade
       Differences among schools
    Design of the Study
       Identification of more and less successful teachers
       Classroom observations
       Educational criticisms
         Procedures
         Identification of successful and comparison teachers
         Securing teacher cooperation
         Classroom observations

Your own qualitative study should contain captions and sub-topics unique to your topic, but the overall logic should be similar. Try your own skeletal version, using the *basic framework for theses or dissertations*. Exclude those captions that are inappropriate and add new ones as needed. Your own qualitative outline will emerge, and when it works, you will feel it!

The study we will use for illustration purposes adheres to two organizational patterns called *Studies of Notable Qualities of Performers* and *Studies of Notable Qualities of Contexts.* Those "organizational patterns" are featured in the companion book to this one, entitled *21 Models for Developing and Completing Theses, Dissertations and Projects*

Three points are noteworthy about this particular dissertation. It involved only four cases observed, and the committee members were three of the most distinguished education professors in America: Eliot Eisner, Nathaniel Gage, and George Politzer, all of Stanford University. The third point is that it required 774 pages!

You should understand that qualitative research resists capture and simple explanation as is possible, say, with quantitative research. Thus, we rely in the remainder of this chapter on "showing not telling" in the hope that readers interested in this "organizational pattern" can be "jump-started" toward successful completion of their scholarly ventures from the excellent example that follows.

With an apology beforehand for the lengthy example below, we will show selected segments. It is important to note the similarities between this qualitative approach and the quantitative example shown earlier. In other words, you should compare the general outline of this study to the *basic framework for theses or dissertations* shown earlier.

A good starting point is an excerpt from Chapter 1 of *Don't Be Teachin' Jovita Wrong: An Exploration of Reading Instruction in Four Urban Third Grade Classrooms*:

CHAPTER 1

THE NATURE OF THE STUDY

This study offers a qualitative description of the activities and exchanges between teachers and Black children in two "ghetto" schools. The people who participated in the study were teachers and students in four third-grade classrooms in compensatory education program schools in the Oakland, California School District in 1977-78. The study was concerned with the question of how classrooms in which inner-city Black children do learn to read differ qualitatively from similar classrooms in which children make little progress in learning to read. Because it sought to discover elements of possible educational significance to a small number of children within...

The overall expectation was that the study would highlight important qualities and characteristics of outstanding urban classrooms as well as those that were less than outstanding. Further, it was hoped that comparisons would provide...

*Remember that it is extremely important to tell the informed reader what **not** to expect.*

In this type of research, clear understanding of the research boundaries is important:

<u>Some Limitations of the Study</u>

The following are possible limitations which should be considered in evaluating the results of this study. The limitations discussed below concern: (1) a basic caution related to correlational research; (2) the interpretation of achievement test data; and (3) the absence of researcher "blindness."

It was noted earlier in this chapter that the study is discovery-oriented, that it focuses on observations directed at description, interpretation, and appraisal of pervasive qualities of classroom life. As such, this study is limited to <u>description</u> of qualities. It cannot claim causal relationships between pervasive qualities and student reading achievement outcomes. Such an assumption of causality would result in the *post hoc* fallacy, in which it is assumed or proposed that one thing causes another since it occurs before the other. (Kerlinger 1973, 279).

Teachers in this study were identified largely on the basis of the relative magnitude of class mean reading achievement scores. A cautionary note on the interpretation of test data is in order. The cauttion concerns the possible influence of regression effects on test scores. Campbell and Stanley (1963, 180-81) suggested that the phenomenon of "regression to the mean," in which extremely low pretest scores...

The very nature of the study, focused as it was on the identification of pervasive qualities in "more successful" and "less successful" classrooms, required identification of such classrooms at the outset of the study and thus virtually precluded researcher "blindess" relative to the identities of "more successful" and "less successful" teachers. While this absence of researcher foreknowledge concerning comparative teacher effectiveness in reading instruction would have been preferable, such "blindness" is impossible because of certain practical problems of the study context. One problem derived from.... Second, the study design required that principal nominations (of "more successful" and "less successful" teachers) be used as a second criterion for teacher identification. The manner in which this aspect interfered with researcher "blindness" is obvious. However, several considerations argue against this as a serious limitation of the study. They are: (1) lack of researcher knowledge of reading achievement ourcomes for the study year; (2) the use of reading achievement as...

Because the organization and development of your Chapter 2 was discussed earlier, we will move on to Chapter 3. Readers should compare the sequence of the Chapter 3 in this example to the one presented earlier.

CHAPTER III

DESIGN AND PROCEDURES OF THE STUDY

This chapter offers a description of the context of the study together with the research design and procedures on which the implementation was based. They are discussed in that order in this chapter.

The Setting of the Study

Classrooms selected for this study were those in the Oakland Unified School District, Oakland, California, during the 1977-78 school year. Oakland, considered a metropolitan center of the San Francisco Bay Area, has a population of approximately 400,000. The ethnicity and economic status of this population roughly coincides with three geographic areas or bands stretching from north to south in Oakland...

The first band----the "flatlands"----is the western areas of the city and spans the edge of San Francisco Bay. It is predominately a Black community. Despite the presence of large industrial...

Spanning the middle section of Oakland, the second band consists of commercial and civic buildings, a lake and a park, large...

Paralleling the ascent of the land from the Bay up to the tall wooded hills at the suburban edge of the city is...

In general, the school enrollment and achievment patterns of Oakland's students parallel the demographic and economic patterns of the city. For example, during the 1977-78 schol year, the total school district enrollment, grades K-12 was 51,761. Approximately 67 percent of these students were Black, 16 percent white. The majority...

Design of the Study

Striking differences in third grade reading achievement patterns at different compensatory education schools suggested the two major research questions of the study. There are several other questions tangential to these, and they will be discussed as they arise.

The first major question was: what are the salient qualities of inner-city classrooms in which children are <u>more</u> successful and those classrooms in ehich children are <u>less</u> successful in learning to read? The second major question was: how do such classrooms differ qualitatively from each other?

Design of the research focused on these questions required: (a) identification of more successful and less successful teachers for comparison purposes, (b) classroom observations of selected teachers, and (c) development of written educational criticisms for individual classrooms together with comparisons of the salient qualities of more successful and less successful classrooms. Each of these aspects is discussed in turn.

The Identification of More Successful and Less Successful Teachers

The rationale for the singular focus on reading achievement of children derives from the needs of inner-city children. It can be argued that there are many other measures----both input and output----for defining teacher "success." This study uses reading achievement as...

At the same school, a less successful (comparison teacher) would beone whose students, while initially...

Classroom Observations

As noted earlier, what is to be considered an adequate amount of observation for classroom study has yet to be determined by educational researchers. The amount of observation for this study was determined by the concern that there be adequate time to permit the observation of recurring

patterns of...

Educational Criticism: The Prime Method of Observation and Study

The final requirement for the study's design was composed of

two parts: the writing of educational criticisms for each of the

observed classrooms and----based on these educational criticisms-

---the development of comparisons between more and less

successful classrooms.

The educational criticisms are focused on the primary

problem of this study: the identification of the salient qualities

of inner-city classrooms in which children are more successful

and those inl which they are less successful in learning to read.

The educational criticisms are intended to offer descriptions and

interpretations of the activities and exchanges within individual

classrooms and, finally, appraisals of those activities and

exchanges. The description and analysis of the individual

classrooms, provided through educational criticism, permitted

work on the study's second research problem: the identification

of qualitative differences between classrooms...

Procedures

The procedures used in carrying out the study design consisted of four broad, sequential steps: the identification of successful and comparison teachers; securing teacher cooperation; classroom observations; and the preparation of educational criticisms, together with classroom comparisons. Detailed descriptions of each follows:

Identification of successful and comparison

Securing Teacher cooperation

Classroom Observations

As to classroom observations, there were three regular third-grade teachers at Whitmore School and, even though only Mrs. Burns and Mrs. Block were the foci of the Whitmore study, all three were observed. This was in keeping with the researcher's stated interest in the whole third grade class.

Two types of observations were conducted in each classroom. The first type, non-participant observation, was done for a minimum of three hours per day over a period of...

A second set of observations were made later in the school year. These were of a more informal nature. The researcher returned to each classroom as a participant (instructional assistant) for a second week (15 hours). This second series of visitations, in addition to repaying the teachers, afforded opportunities for...

In all, the observer spent approximately 30 hours in each classroom. Additional observations and conversations were obtained before school, on the playground, in lunchroom visits with the children and teachers, and through attendance at school programs.

The Educational Criticisms

Educational criticisms offering qualitative description, interpretation, and appraisal of the underlying individual classrooms are presented in Chapter 4. Four sets of data----audiotapes, transcripts, field notes and summary notes developed during the week of non-participant observation, and anecdotal notes from the second week of participant observation were used in writing the educational criticisms for each classroom. Drawn from...

The Comparison of Classrooms

The educational criticisms provide the basis for discussion of apparent qualitative differences between classrooms...

Summary

You should remember that both quantitative and qualitative theses or dissertations use the same *general* pattern of organization or *basic framework for theses or dissertations*. Chapter 2 presents the greatest organizational challenge because of the abundance of literature in most content areas. Although it is difficult to generalize about Chapter 2, you should remember four points. One is that the literature selected should "paint a picture for uninvolved readers. Another is that Chapter 2 should start with a historical overview of the background of the problem. A third is that the literature review should address controverial points, arguments and dichotomies. Fourth, the literature review should cover, explain and defend any concepts, constructs or instruments devised by the writer.

TIP BOX 3: A CALENDAR FOR COMPLETING YOUR THESIS OR DISSERTATION

Think of your thesis or dissertation as a four-part venture. Those parts are (1) exhaustive *background* research; (2) data-gathering as you complete the first three chapters; (3) data analysis; and (4) completion of chapters 4, 5, and all end matter.

Part I: Exhaustive background research

1. Much of the research you conducted for your proposal will be helpful in writing Chapter 1. The background portrait of Chapter 1 should (a) make credible the conceptual hypotheses on which you base your study; and (b) make the case for your *Significance of the Study* section

2. Direct the remainder of the background search to the content of Chapter 2, *Review of Related Literature* and Chapter 3, *Methodology*.

TIP BOX 3 (continued)

3. Review Chapter 6 of this book. Take note of page 130, *About the Content and Organization of Chapter 2.*

Part II: Data-gathering and completing the first three chapters

1. You should conduct your study as you write the first three chapters. Doing so will save considerable time. There exist no reasons to stop writing as you await questionnaire returns, interview outcomes, observational analyses and other data-gathering activities. Report these outcomes in Chapter IV.

2. Review **TIP BOX** 4, pages 181-82, before developing questionnaires or conducting data-gathering activities.

3. Send a draft copy of your first three chapters to your chairperson. There is a strong possibility that your chairperson will approve them and instruct you to send copies to other members of your faculty advisory committee.

4. Develop a system for organizing and presenting collected data. Review pages 94-103 for ideas about this task.

Data Analysis

Remember that data analysis employs both quantitative and qualitative methods. You must conduct data analysis in light of the central interests of your study. It is helpful to *periodically refer to your conceptual hypotheses as you organize your approach to data analysis.*

Completion of chapters 4, 5, and all end matter.

1. Review Chapter 3 of this book related to chapters 4 and 5.

2. Remember that appendixes, charts, illustrations and other end matter must *explicitly illustrate and amplify* points made in your study. "Padding" only serves to detract from the quality of your study.

7

CHAPTERS 4, 5 AND FINIS!

Chapters 4 and 5 constitute the essence of any Master's or doctoral study, because these two chapters contain the outcomes of the study. However, many academicians and prestige accreditation agencies contend that the total process of writing terminal scholarly documents is far more important. They argue that the required intellectual honesty, independence of thought, intensive research, accurate reportage, and high-level skills of discourse serve the highest ends of the university, irrespective of study outcomes.

There are significant differences in quantitative and qualitative studies as presented in chapters 4 and 5. Examples in this chapter explore those differences.

Reportage of the important findings of a study is the central concern of Chapter 4. Although it is impossible to offer a formula for organizing Chapter 4, several general guidelines are helpful.

You should remember that Chapter 4 is for simple reportage of findings, while Chapter 5 is for presentation of conclusions, implications and recommendations for further study. When writing Chapter 4, many students make the mistake of including some of the proper content of Chapter 5.

> *Chapter 4 should present results in an organized manner. Without drawing conclusions, it articulates between hypotheses and conclusions, and reports both confirming and disconfirming results.*

A few general guidelines apply to the organization and development of Chapter 4 of theses and dissertations. Because of the great variation in the content and character of terminal scholarly studies, none of these guidelines might be applicable to any specific study. Thus, you should observe the points made below as general reminders about the proper organization of most theses and dissertations:

The organization and format of Chapter 4 should adhere to the order in which hypotheses, questions or ideas are introduced in the main body of the study.

In Chapter 1, most studies identify one or several conceptual hypotheses which led to or stimulated them. Frequently, you must convert these conceptual hypotheses to null form in Chapter 3, in certain studies. In the absence of any other organizational criteria, you should discuss the findings related to each hypothesis in the *exact order* in which the hypotheses were introduced in Chapter 1.

Let's look at an example of this, using an excerpt from Chapter 1 of a fictitious thesis entitled *A Five Year Analysis of the Impact of Year-'Round Education Schedules on Math Scores and Selected Attitude Indicators*:

Conceptual Hypotheses

The basic hypotheses that stimulated this study were that (1) the overall mathematics capability of students who complete the kindergarten to sixth grade on a *New Concept* calendar and those who complete traditional kindergarten to sixth grade calendars would not show meaningful differences in measured achievement over a relatively long time interval; and (2) schools organized on the *New Concept* calendar would not lead to improved teacher, parent and student outcomes in the affective domain. Expressed in the form of specific conceptual hypotheses which are offered here as well as appropriately translated in Chapter 3 in null form where they are discussed in the context of the research design of the study, these research interests are, respectively:

Conceptual Hypothesis 1:   Comparative mathematics achievement in selected grade levels between traditional and *New Concept* schools will reflect no...

Conceptual Hypothesis 2: *New Concept* schools, operated over a five-year interval between 1988 and 1993:

(a) will not elicit discernible differences in teacher satisfaction as originally anticipated and reflected in...

(b) will not elicit discernible improvements in parent attitudes toward school as originally anticipated and reflected in school board minutes...

> *Hypotheses are nothing more than informed statements of hunches about relationships between elements in your study*

Now, let's look forward to see how these hypotheses influence the organization of Chapter 4:

Chapter 4

Analysis of Findings

Findings related to the present study are reported below, in the exact order in which they were presented as conceptual hypotheses in Chapter 1 and as corresponding null hypotheses in Chapter 3. Those findings are related to whether (1) there are differences in mathematics achievement in *New Concept* and traditional schools in selected grade levels; and (2) schools organized on the *New Concept* calendar would lead to improved teacher and parent outcomes in the affective domain.

Findings Related to Null Hypothesis 1

The rationale for use of the Chi Square I statistic was offered in Chapter 3. Specific data and computational outcomes are offered below.

Specifically, the annual mathematics performance of third and fifth graders in traditional schools was held as the expected standard and the five-year performance of *New Concept* schools was held as the observed standard (or frequencies). The statistical design, performed for each of the five years for each grade level of concern, is demonstrated in Table 1 below.

Table 1
Third Grade Raw Score Means, Mathematics,
1988-89 School Year

	School 1	School 2	School 3
Traditional	611.7	634.0	636.1
Concept 6	637.0	638.1	605.7

Obtained Chi Square $= 2.51$, $df = 2$, $\alpha = .05$
Tabled   Chi Square $= 5.99$

Conclusion: Retain the null hypothesis: there were no significant differences in third grade mathematics achievement score means between traditional and *New Concept* schools for the 1988-1989 school year.

You should continue this approach, reporting the statistical outcomes for both third and fifth grade over the five-year time interval, thus completing the statistical findings related to Hypothesis 1. Then, the focus turns to Hypothesis 2:

Findings Related to Hypothesis 2

Examination of findings related to Conceptual Hypothesis 2(a) proceeded through analysis of the following documents: School board minutes, parent and teacher surveys, Year-Round Education Committee minutes, and similar documentation. In

1989, the original Year-Round Committee recommended *New Concept* for the following reasons: to provide common calendars for....

In the school board minutes from the next school board meeting, 7 December 1993, Ms. _____, representing the Teachers' Association, spoke to correct a possible misconception about...

In a parent and teacher survey taken in 1991, 70 percent of 347 teachers polled at random elected to remain on *New Concept* as opposed to returning to a four-track calendar if this...

In an interview with ____ _____, Director of Year Round Education, the question was asked as to why the high schools went off *New Concept.* She stated that the reason...

Thorough examination of all of the qualitative information and data above led to the finding that Conceptual Hypothesis 2a could be supported, as there were no discernible differences in teacher satisfaction in *New Concept* as originally anticipated or as expressed by...

The point should be clear by now.   Got it? You should maintain this pattern throughout Chapter 4.

Additional relevant findings must be reported in Chapter 4, together with other aspects of the study with which they are associated.   Major additional relevant unanticipated findings deserve separate mention and clarification.

Frequently,   you   encounter   additional   important unanticipated findings during the course of your research. You should report them (1) together with other associated findings or aspects of the study; and (2) in the order in which those findings are reported.

When a questionnaire or test instrument constitutes the major portion of research results, an effective format for organization of Chapter 4 is one based on the *exact* format and sequence of the instrument.

This means that you can use the *exact questionnaire format* as a framework for reporting the combined, collated results in Chapter 4. We will illustrate this important point with the fictitious thesis example introduced in the previous chapter: *A Statewide Assessment of School Principals' Knowledge of Attention Deficits Disorders (A.D.D.) and Related School Problems.* The example below illustrates a way of reporting the results, as well as selected segments of the *collated* (fictional) questionnaire used.

CHAPTER 4

Analysis of the Findings

This chapter is organized on the basis of the presentation of a

composite response of respondents to the survey instrument used

in the study (Appendix B). The composite response is

organized *seriatim* on the basis of the responses as they appeared

in the survey instrument. The only deviation from this sequence

is that the demographic data (items 26-36) are presented first

because they give the reader a conceptual backdrop as to the composite character, experience and other demographic data

related to the respondents.

The collated questionnaire which follows is presented in the

exact order of the original questionnaire as sent to respondents.

All numbers in boldface are those of actual respondents to

catetgories on the questionnaire.

The Collated Questionnaire

SA   A   N   D   SD

1. A.D.D. students' speech errors should be corrected frequently
in order to improve their pronunciation

8   45   22   93   37

8.   When A.D.D. students....

19. An urgent inservice need in all schools is immediate
training of teachers in problematic aspects of children with
A.D.D.

104   81   6   12   2

PART II

1. Your years' experience in site level administration   0 - 3
4 - 6   7 -10   11 -15   15+

29   44   76   51   5

2. Your years' teaching prior to administration are   0 - 5
6 - 10   11-15   16-20   20+

6   28   93   74   4

3. Your years assigned to present site as principal are...

Following your complete presentation of the collated questionnaire or instrument, you should present a factual analysis of the outcomes, without interpretations or meanings. Here is an example of such an analysis:

Demographic Data

The demographic data are reported in tables 6-16 (Appendix D, pp. 80-84). This data provides background information about the sites in the study as well as background information about respondents. Of a total of 300 surveys mailed, 208 were returned and 3 were returned incomplete. Of all returns, 205 were valid for use in the study. 92 were not returned. This resulted in a 68 percent rate, even with two follow-up mailings.

The population from which the sample was selected included schools with at least 500 A.D.A. elementary, 800 A.D.A. middle school, and 1200 A.D.A. high school. Some respondents were non-principals. Of these, 10 were vice-principals, 5 were coordinators of categorical programs, 2 were department chairs, and 6 were school counselors, probably assigned the task of responding to the survey.

Composite Scores for Related Items

Composite scores for clusters of related items were reported in Table 19 (Appendix E, p. 88). It was noted that lower mean scores had greater variance than higher mean scores. This may indicate a relative lack of consensus in those areas with lower scores.

Findings Related to the Statistical Test

The frequency distributions were analyzed using the Chi-Square I (Goodness of Fit) test. All computations involved comparisons of obtained distributions with expected distributions of no preferences.

Items 5 and 16 varied significantly from the expected distribution at the .05 level at 4*df*. The remaining items all differed significantly at .01 or .001 levels of significance. Scores for items 3, 5, and 15 were below the expected distributions, but for all other items the scores exceed expected responses as defined. Table 20 (Appendix F, p. 90) summarized the Chi-Square values for opinionnaire items.

A look at Chapter 4 of a qualitative study. Let's return to *Don't Be Teachin' Jovita Wrong: An Exploration of Reading Instruction in Four Urban Third Grade Classrooms,* the qualitative study used in the previous chapter. Remember that *content* dictates the organizational pattern of qualitative studies. In that dissertation, the Chapter 4 outline was:

Chapter IV - The Milieu of the Classrooms of Mrs. Burns,
Miss Block, Mrs. Sutter, and Mrs. Ruffell

The Milieu of the Classrooms
    At Whitmore School
    At Gillespie School
    The Differences

The Approach to Classroom Description
    Mrs. Burns' Class: The schoolroom, reading, language
        arts, and physical configurations.
    Miss Block's Class: The schoolroom,
        reading, language arts, and physical configurations.

Comparing the Classrooms
    The framework for comparisons
        Qualities: Similarities, differences and unique
            qualities.
    Mrs. Sutter's Class: The schoolroom, reading, language
        arts, and physical configurations.
    Mrs. Ruffell's Class: The schoolroom, reading, language
        arts, and physical configurations.
Comparing the Classrooms
    The framework for comparisons
    Qualities: Similarities, differences and unique qualities.

---

*Extended dialogue is appropriate and quite common in Chapter
4 of theses and dissertations using qualitative inquiry. Such
dialogue does much to capture the ambience of the study context
and illustrate bases for the findings and conclusions of the
investigator.*

This is a commonsense outline. The study describes the
context (milieu) first. Next, the framework for description is
detailed. Finally, each classroom is analyzed on the basis of
that framework. The actual writing from a small segment of
that outline chapter is instructive:

<u>Mrs. Burns' Class</u>

Mrs. B:	Is that right?
Kids:	Yeah!
Mrs. B:	Is that right, Monica?
Monica:	Yeah.
Mrs. B:	Is that right, John?
John:	Yeah.
Mrs. B:	I want you to tell me if that's not right. I don't want to teach Eric wrong, Jovita wrong. Her mother could come up here and get me!

<u>The Schoolroom</u>

At quarter to nine, denim pantsuit a blur, three-inch heels clattering as she takes the stairs two at a time, Mrs. Burns is within earshot of her audience as she shouts, "It's going to be a tremendous day! We're going to learn a lot today!" Marvey, Michael Williams, and Toya, who have been sitting on the floor outside the classroom, scramble to their feet as Mrs. Burns...

WELCOME TO WHITMORE SCHOOL bid the foot-tall letters of a banner. Somber and playful pairs of eyes keep watch. On the west wall, old prints show old, bent Black women hoeing a field. Over there on the north wall, a huge, pebbly surfaced yellow Tweety Bird stares down at the kids. Legs dangling down from atop a tall cabinet, their arms entwined around a flower pot and its droopy philodendron, Black Raggedy Ann dolls silently...

Mrs. Burns and the children head for the far corner to the teacher's desk squeezed between the ditto worksheet storage tower and the long work table. Goldtone trophies rise above the clutter of teachers' manuals (at least one each for reading, math, spelling, language, science, health) and teachers' plan books on Mrs. Burns' desk. Seated at her desk, Mrs. Burns collects lunch money from...

Michael Williams (there are three Michaels in Room 21, so each one is called by both first and last names) lowers the brown shades... Ready for the day to begin, the board is filled with sets of today's assignments in reading, reading workbooks, math, language and spelling. The first set of assignments is for the "lowest" group---the "Level 7's"; and the second set is for...

Four rows of eight lift-top desks fill up the room. A child's name is printed in Black letters on the front of each: Kevin, Derrick, Ellen, John... The names are printed again on the big objectives chart, and it seems almost everyone had completed...

Reading

It is almost nine o'clock and time for the reading period to begin. Three kinds of work are done each reading period: vocabulary drill, word study, and oral reading. We start where class begins every morning: vocabulary drill.

Drill and Practice with Mrs. Burns. The "9 O'Clockers" and most of the "10 O'Clockers" are in the room, taking care of early morning business. Michael Williams and Kevin (self-appointed custodians of basketballs) dribble the balls from their overnight desk hiding places to the cloakroom----all is ready for recess. The ten o'clock girls pull desks into a semi-circle at the board...

    9:00   (*Not looking in their direction, saying nothing to the children, Mrs. Burns positions herself. wooden pointer in hand next to the vocabulary poster on which 36 words from the Level 7 reader are printed. Chatter and milling around cease as, hearing her "whoas" and "Oh, ohs" the kids rush over to the "Vocabulary Corner" bumping into each other as they jostle for position around teacher and poster.*

Mrs. B: Now I want to see how many you people have <u>mastered</u>. It's about time we take this vocabulary list down and put up another one. *(There is foot shuffling as kids angle for position----but there is no talking.* We got all these words?

Class: Yeah!

Mrs. B: *(Looking directly at them).* Let's see how many <u>have</u> these words today. No matter how I jump around----Troy, I know you can't see, baby. Michael Langworth, I know your eyes are going to be all lopsided, all lopsided. How many people know these words? How many have all these words down 'pat' so that pretty soon I can put up a new list? Can you see, Tracy? Why don't you come around here behind...scoot your seat. O.K. Everybody ready? Where is Rewia? *(Rewia, sitting there, off in his own world, jumps at the sound of his name).* Everybody ready? We have to wait for anybody? Everybody awake and ready to go? Ready?

Class: Yeah!

Mrs. B: *(All eyes are on the poster and she is satisfied that they are with her.)* O.K., here we go! *(As she points at "value," "repair," "sense" the whole class yells the words. But they are not crisp enough for her).*

Don't sing them! Say them sharply and get it over with. O.K!

(They call out each word as she rapidly skips around the poster to "beneath"."beside," and "defend." Abruptly, the routine changes.)

O.K. Gregory----right around in this row down to Leo. You guys ready? Know what I'm talking about?

<u>What the Drill Does</u>. Clearly, the vocabulary drill (a small but consistent element of Mrs. Burns' instruction) has a managerial function----it starts the day off crisply. It also has a two-fold instructional function: (1) to enhance vocabulary development, because the words are not basic sigh words of the

Dolch 220 variety; rather they are the most difficult "enrichment" words from the Level 7 reader; and (2) to develop "automaticity" in recognition of these words: in seven minutes, 36 vocabulary words (pronunciation and meaning) are reviewed three times----as they have been reviewed each day for the past month. Practice, reinforcement, "overlearning" of the words until the children have them in ther permanent word repertoires is the expected result. Who, after a month of this, will fail to recognize the words, their pronunciations and their meanings?

Note that the research method in operation in this example combines ethnographic and case study methods. The central interest in such studies is copious documentation or "thick description" of teaching and learning activity in each scenario so that subsequent analysis can reveal or "tease out" those things that work. However, should reserve Chapter 5 for interpretations, meanings, and implications.

That should help those of you who have trouble organizing Chapter 4. Feel free to use this approach in your own ventures in organizing Chapter 4, when appropriate. Try out the sample language provided here for getting "jump-started" in your own writing!

The central concern of Chapter 5 of theses or dissertations is comprehensive explanation of the important meanings, implications for practice, and new directions for further study. It is the proper context for expression of the *defensible* conclusions, opinions, attitudes and beliefs of the author.

Although many variations are permissible, the usual or standard title of Chapter 5 is *Summary, Conclusions,*

Implications and Recommendations. Irrespective of what actual title you use for the chapter, it is a good idea to discuss its content in the order suggested by that standard title.

> *In addition to summarizing your study, Chapter 5 should draw conclusions based on (1) facts and (2) connections between original questions, hypotheses, and results.*

Before moving to illustrations, you should note one more important aspect. For the first time during the development of your thesis or dissertation, *you can express your opinions.* However, you should only express opinions that you can defend on the basis of (1) relevant theories, constructs, concepts and ideas from the related literature; (2) examples from actual practice; or (3) accepted principles of scholarly argument. This means that you should offer your opinions cautiously and only when you can defend them.

You should address the *Summary* portion first, in as few words as possible. Let's use as an example the fictitious thesis discussed earlier, *The Impact of New Concept Year-'Round Education Schedules on Math Scores and Selected Attitude Indicators, 1998-1993* :

Chapter 5

Summary, Conclusions, Implications and

Recommendations for Further Study

Within this final chapter, various defensible conclusions and implications were offered. Following these, several recommendations for further study were offered in concise form, in the interest of providing meaningful directions for subsequent researchers in the area.

Summary

This study attempted to determine whether there existed meaningful, sustained, educationally significant differences in student mathematics performance levels between K-6 *New Concept* schools and those organized on traditional calendars, as anticipated and projected by those who advocated year-round education. The group opposed to *New Concept* had generated much animosity and controversy. Although both the district administration and...

However, the literature review conducted in Chapter 2 revealed clearly that few studies have been done regarding academic achievement in *New Concept* schools; and virtually all motives for year-round calendars centered on relief of overcrowding.

The present study was a qualitative and quantitative examination of the academic achievement of students educated under both traditional and *New Concept* calendars in the district. It was undertaken to provide orderly, defensible data that would offer a basis for...

The following are the major, educationally relevant findings that resulted from the present study, listed in relation to the original conceptual hypotheses posited in the first chapter:

New Concept mathematics scores were significantly higher for third grade for four of the five years between 1989 and 1993. For fifth grade during the same time interval, there were no significant differences in mathematics achievement of...

Discernible differences in teacher satisfaction in *New Concept* year-round education were not elicited as originally anticipated and reflected in school board minutes, surveys, Year-Round Education Committee minutes and other documentation. Discernible differences in parent satisfaction were not elicited as originally anticipated...

There were several additional findings of note in this study. First of all, the...

Conclusions

The foremost conclusion drawn from this study is that *New Concept* has a "no harm done" effect on mathematics achievement in the district. This finding supported similar results found in other studies of *New Concept* in Beaumont, Texas, San Bernardino, California, and Tonopah, Nevada. These result were discussed in Chapter 2.

The current study, as well as the literature, seems to indicate that although there generally were slight achievement differences favoring *New Concept* schools, there were no signifiant differences...

Another explanation might be that teachers cut out many extras such as holiday parties or "free time" in order to effectively use...

One other conclusion might be that the two-month vacation blocks might actually be instrumental for student retention of academic skills and concepts. The former three-month vacation break was often blamed for...

Teacher satisfaction may have resulted from the fact that teachers, contrary ro some claims, realized their students were learning and retaining knowledge while on...

Finally, perhaps the reason for the discontent of the citizens' group was, simply, fear of change. Since so few studies have been done on *New Concept* achievement, people may not have been ready to give up "school as they knew it" for something so different. The unhappy teachers and parents...

Implications for Practice and Practitioners

The findings of this study suggest that school districts may safely implement *New Concept* calendars when seeking to improve housing capacity for elementary students. The fewer number of days on the *New Concept* calendar does not seem to result in lower test scores compared to...

Regarding parent satisfaction, it was obvious by studying parent surveys that the prime concern of parents was not length of the school year. Rather, these parents wanted to retain the neighborhood school concept and common calendars for...

Districts considering the implementation of *New Concept* should learn from this study that community education prior to the adoption of altered calendars is critically important. Publication of studies...

Recommendations for Further Study

1. Another comparative study of *New Concept* and traditional schools should take place in the same school district, using Reading scores on the Comprehensive Tests of Basic Skills (CTBS).

2. A similar study should be conducted comparing two different grades in....

3. A study should be conducted on the benefit of longer school days, as compared to a longer school year.

4. A similar study should be conducted comparing student achievement of seventh and eighth grade *New Concept* students and those attending under traditional calendars.

5. Finally, an important study focused on...

You must base the Conclusions in Chapter 5 of your thesis or dissertation on facts collected in your study. You must also relate to the original study questions and state explicitly whether study outcomes supported your research hypotheses.

Here is another look at Chapter 5, using another fictitious topic introduced earlier, *A Statewide Assessment of School Principals' Knowledge of Attention Deficits Disorders (A.D.D.) and Related School Problems.* An additional perspective on the organization of Chapter 5 might be helpful.

CHAPTER 5

Summary, Conclusions, Implications
and Recommendations

The major purposes of this study were to provide answers to several research questions:

1. What is the extent of knowledge or conceptual grasp of California principals relative to serving the instructional needs of A.D.D. diagnosed students?

2. To what extent are principals prepared to effectively evaluate teachers in the context of instruction of A.D.D. diagnosed students?

3. What aspects of academic and professional backgrounds of respondent principals appear associated with enhanced knowledge and awareness of the techniques and dynamics of providing quality education to A.D.D. diagnosed students?

4.   What are the needs for further professional growth and development for principals in the above areas?

Chapter 5 is oriented to presentation of conclusions based on the data analysis reported in Chapter 4.

Conclusions

The response to Question (2) above was provided by reviewing the number of surveys that were delegated to non-principals, the amount of specialized training received by respondents, and the responses to the A.D.D. opinionnaire items.

Approximately 21.89% of respondents delegated the survey to another...

Responses to Questions (1) and (3) above were provided by examination of the opinionnaire items which pertained to effective instruction of A.D.D. diagnosed learners. The responses to these items revealed the following opinions of respondents (see Table 17, Appendix E, p. 86):

1. Correction of speech errors should not be done frequently.

2. Instruction should be presented in context, through the use of visual props, manipulatives and concrete objects.

3.   Affective factors are critical for effective instruction of A.D.D. diagnosed learners.

4. Audio-lingual methods are highly effective.

Responses for these items endorsed established A.D.D. teaching principles in four of the seven items (1, 2, 6 and 7). There were contradictory responses to items involving...

Implications

This study revealed that a significant proportion of principals delegate their responsibility for instructional leadership and administration of activities germane to A.D.D. diagnosed learners. While delegation may be a necessity in many aspects of high school operation, decisions related to effective program modification can only be made by an informed principal and...

There is a need for widespread, comprehensive training of principals in all aspects of the education of A.D.D....

Recommendations for Further Study

The lack of content area specialists informed in educational strategies for A.D.D. learners in higher level classes should be studied. What conditions might induce these specialists to...

Instructional competency of teachers for A.D.D. diagnosed learners should be examined. What programmatic needs do teachers perceive at their school sites for improved teaching of A.D.D. diagnosed learners? What is the level of administrative support...

A future study should survey postgraduate programs. To what

extent are these programs preparing principals to provide leadership

in instruction for A.D.D. diagnosed learners? At the university

level, should such training be included in credential programs...

Chapter 5 should present implications for practice in your study area. Implications should be presented if (a) they are clearly implied from the findings, (b) if they are reasonably consistent with other theories,(c) if they are presented concisely, and (d) if they are presented cautiously, clearly identified as speculation only.

How should you organize Chapter 5 of a qualitative study? "Showing" is important here. Selected sections of Chapter 5 of the study entitled *Don't Be Teachin' Jovita Wrong: An Exploration of Reading Instruction in Four Urban Third Grade Classrooms* might be quite revealing in the sense that they could offer ideas for researchers interested in pursuing this "organizational pattern" in other fields. Let's look at a few sections of this chapter.

CHAPTER V

QUALITY OF INSTRUCTION: EXPLORING THE ELUSIVE

This project began with the simple but, as _____(1973)

called it, "cosmic" question: how do classrooms in which children

are learning to read differ from classrooms in which children make little progress in learning to read? Pursuit of the question has involved a number of processes.

The first was exploration of individual classrooms, two more successful and two less so. The purpose of the explorations was...

Because the work of Chapter Four was essentially exploratory---as qualities became apparent they were described----that chapter could have no organizational "theme." The criticisms, for the most part, took their shape from the observations. In contrast, this chapter is written from a specific point of view. As the title indicates, its organizing theme is identification of possible components of the quality of instruction. The concept and the reason for its selection as focal point require some elaboration.

<u>With Time on Task: The Quality of Instruction</u>

As a result of the work of several theorists and researchers, the issue of time in the classroom has received considrerable study recently. The essential message of this work is that if students are able to spend the amount of time they <u>need</u> to learn a particular skill, they will learn it; more time spent on-task in learning is...

Several models of school learning (_____1963; _____ and _____1975...

...

The remainder of this chapter consists of two sections. The first offers analyses of the more successful and comparison classrooms and, on the basis of the analyses of their differences, recommendations for further study. The second section, offering a conceptualization of quality of instruction, presents the conclusions of this study.

Comparing the Classrooms: Exploration of the Components of Quality of Instruction

Exploration of the components of the quality of instruction centers on comparison of the two more successful classrooms with the two less successful classrooms in five broad areas: time, curriculum content, methods, noise and milieu.

In the same manner as occurred in the two-classroom comparisons, the similar-different-unique patterns appear when the two pairs of more successful and less successful classrooms are compared. A few qualities in all four classrooms appear to be the same. There are also qualities of Mrs. Burns' and Mrs. Sutter's classrooms that are alike but different from those of... There are also some qualities that remain unique to a single teacher.

Essentially, this project is exploratory and its central purpose is identification and description of important qualities and constituents of more successful and less successful classrooms that <u>may</u> be related to reading achievement. Therefore, its recommendations cannot be statements of what teachers should or should not do to improve reading instruction. Rather, recommendations are limited to suggestions of what may be productive areas for further study. These recommendations are presented as "Candidates for Further Study" at the conclusion of each section of classroom comparisons. The comparisons begin with the matter of time in the classroom.

<u>Time</u>

Currently there is much research indicating that time----both the amount simply allocated to instruction and the amount of time students are actively engaged with academic tasks----is correlated with achievement. While logical,...

<u>Allocated Time</u>. The most obvious difference between the classrooms is the allocation of time. More successful teachers allocate 120 minutes a day to reading. Comparison teachers allocate only 60 minutes. The differences in allocated time...

<u>Engaged Time</u>. Even when differences in allocated time are accounted for, large disparities in time for reading instruction still exist. They are due to the substantial differences between successful and comparison classrooms in the amount of time...

The nature of the differences is suggested by the descriptors of the quality of time in the four classrooms. In the more successful classrooms "Being in Gear" (Mrs. Burns) and "Doing a Processional March" (Mrs. Sutter) suggest a steady task-orientation in the use of classroom time (although the pace of time and activities in Mrs. Burns' room is more lively). These qualities contrast starkly with those of the comparison rooms: "Good Days and Bad Days" (Block) and "No Press-No Stress" (Ruffell)---- descriptors intended to indicated the inconsistent, often fragmentary time on task in reading.

Student engagement time (attending to tasks at hand) rates in Mrs. Burns' and Mrs. Sutter's rooms are consistently good...

<u>Candidates for Further Study</u>

...More successful teachers believe in using the language arts period for reading skills practice; comparison teachers do not. This accounts for substantial time differences. However...

These two factors suggest that researchers in reading instruction need to look at:

1. How are language arts periods as well as reading periods used?

2. In classrooms with a language arts rather than a strict reading orientation to language arts instruction, how well are language activities done?

In addition to study of the kinds of things children are doing when they are engaged with their reading tasks, insight into the use of time might be provided by asking

3. What kinds of things are children doing when they are not engaged with academic work?

Curriculum Content

Examined in this section are three curriculum-relevant aspects of the classrooms. The content and emphasis of reading instruction are considered first. Subsequent discussion deals with...

You should present Recommendations for Further Study in Chapter 5. Recommendations should focus on important aspects not covered because of limitations on the scope of your study, as well as broader questions that need answers.

About Thematic Analysis. At this point, many of you might wonder about the *method* used by the qualitative researcher in the previous example. Possibly the only generalization that can be made about such a method is that it is a search for *sustained themes, behaviors* and *actions*---in the present instance, in the teaching approaches of the two effective teachers.

Such a qualitative researcher starts from an extremely well informed knowledge base about whatever is being observed. This means that such a qualitative researcher could not begin research without a firm conceptual grasp of the meaning of effective teaching.

After repeated observations of each teacher accompanied by copious note-taking, the researcher is finally confronted with the task of making sense out of what has been observed. At such a point, the researcher has on hand the notes made and the memories of various observations.

The *informed* search backward through notes and memory is a look for *sustained effective behaviors* or *consistent strands* or *themes* in the teaching of each teacher observed. The sustained themes can and often do lead to cautious generalizations about what seems to be effective. Certainly, when sustained themes are found among several teachers, the generalizations are strengthened.

Another way of saying this is that such a research "method" involves *thematic analysis*. Since the increased popularity of qualitative research in the past two decades, ethnographic interviews, observations and other qualitative information-gathering approaches are fairly common. However, you must analyze the information. Although there are several approaches for doing so, thematic analysis might be one of the most effective for achieving the desired ends of the study illustrated above. Here is a definite procedure for performing a thematic analysis:

1. Collect the data from all sources.

2. Combine and catalogue related patterns into themes and sub-themes.

4. Look for emergingpatterns, then seek feedback about them from informants and sources.

5. On the basis of field literature and contextual knowledge, build an argument for choosing the themes (Review the example above, *Don't Be Teachin' Jovita Wrong: An Exploration of Reading Instruction in Four Urban Third Grade Classrooms*).

Summary

When organizing Chapter 4, you should adhere to the sequence or order in which hypotheses, questions or ideas occur in the main body of the study. Report additional important findings in Chapter 4. When your study involves a questionnaire, organize Chapter 4 on the *exact* format and sequence of that questionnaire.

Chapter 5 focuses on comprehensive explanation of the important meanings, implications for practice, and new directions for further study surfaced by a study. Chapter 5 presents the first opportunity during the thesis or dissertation for expressing your opinions. You must defend your opinions on the basis of (1) relevant theories, constructs, concepts and ideas from the related literature; (2) examples from actual practice; (3) principles of scholarly argument and (4) common sense. This means that you should only offer your opinions when you can defend them.

TIP BOX 4: ADVANTAGES OF SCALED RESPONSE FORMATS

During your literature search related to field problems, you might run into results of opinion polls based on scaled response formats. You might find several items exactly like those you intend to include in your questionnaire. .Such polls frequently present responses on a Likert scale, with actual numbers of respondents in each category. *When you also use Likert scales, you set yourself up for making immediate and direct statistical comparisons of your research to existent research.* Three possibilities are:

1. Testing divergence of obtained distributions from values (distributions) calculated on the hypothesis of equal probability.

2. Testing divergence of obtained distributions from values (distributions) reported by organizations or other researchers.

3. Testing divergence of obtained distributions from values (distributions) calculated on the hypothesis of a normal distribution.

The statistical comparisons in (1) and (3) are *always available*, while comparisons in situation (2) depend on the existence of similar research. Suppose your survey reveals the following distribution of responses to the statement:

20. Teachers should have at least 4 semester units of coursework related to effective teaching of A.D.D. diagnosed students

S A	A	N	D	S D
23	18	24	17	18

First, you might be interested in determining whether your obtained distribution is significantly different from a distribution where there are *no* preferences, as in (1) above:

S A	A	N	D	S D
20	20	20	20	20

The Chi-Square (X^2) Goodness of Fit statistic offers a good test of the similarity or divergence of the two distributions. In this case, an obtained Chi-Square value of 2.10 (4 df) reveals no significant differences. This would *encourage* a conclusion that the responses you obtained on that item revealed no clear preferences. You could perform similar calculations for all items presented in the same Likert format. When you are building a consensus model, these calculations yield *clear bases for decisions about aspects that you*

TIP BOX 4 (Continued)

should include in your model. Suppose you were writing the thesis, *An Experience-Based Procedural Model for Selection, Training and Placement of Bilingual Hispanic Teacher Aides.* If your questionnaire yielded the following distribution of responses on the item

20. First priority in selection should go to those aides who live in the school neighborhood.

S A	A	N	D	S D
31	33	26	7	3

Comparison to a distribution of no preferences would yield highly significant differences, resulting in confidence about incorporating the results of that response into your model. You can also compare your obtained distribution, *question by question*, to a distribution reported by a professional organization or researcher, as in (2) above. Suppose such a response distribution to the same statement, reported in a professional journal, was

S A	A	N	D	S D
29	22	16	18	15

This reveals that the null hypothesis of no significant differences must be retained. You can also compare your obtained distribution to a *normal distribution,* using the Chi Square I statistic. Divide the baseline of a normal curve into five equal segments of $1.2s$ each; then calculate the proportions of the normal distribution found in each segment of the curve, using a table of areas under the curve

Between   3s and 1.80s = .035   1.8s and .6s = .24
                  .6s and -6s = .45   -6s and -1.8s = .24
              -1.8s and -3s = .035

c. Multiply each proportion by 100 (or the total number of responses in your sample returns) to find the actual number in each response category:

S A	A	N	D	S D
3.5	24	45	24	3.5

d. Calculate Chi Square I, using this normal distribution and your obtained distribution.

8

A PROJECT MIGHT BE A BETTER ALTERNATIVE FOR *YOU*

We have focused on theses and dissertations in this book because they are standard requirements of most colleges and universities. We will now use this chapter to focus on projects, which some colleges accept as terminal scholarly research activities for the Master's degree.

Two considerations determine whether you should you pursue a project instead of a thesis. First, you should complete a *thesis* if you intend to get a doctorate later. Frequently, professors in quality institutions like to see your thesis before deciding to work with you. Projects generally do not "sell" as well in such situations. Second, you should complete a project if that project can be used as an entree to employment in your specialized field of interest. An example is a pilot film that you might use to illustrate your competence in directing or film-making. Another is music or a musical arrangement written for a show. A third is a computer program for optimization of input-output relationships between, say, school district program expenditures and measured outcomes.

Possibilities are limited only by field needs and your special interests.   Sincere interest in your project is important, as it will spur you on to completion.

Projects always involve development of *products* usable in specific geographical areas, communities, school districts, hospitals and other agencies.

In Chapter 1, we noted that generalizability was the major difference between *projects* and *theses*. Projects are usable in specific areas, communities, school districts, hospitals and other organizations with similar demographic conditions.

Typically, projects are manuals, guidelines, directories and other *products* immediately useful and applicable to certain agencies. For example, in a school district a project might be *A Procedural Manual for Hiring, Training and Assigning Bilingual Hispanic Instructional Aides in San Joaquin County Schools.* On the other hand, a corresponding thesis might be *A Model for Effective Employment of Bilingual Hispanic Aides..* Similarly, in a public water district a project might be *A Three-Month Procedure for Maximizing Watershed Containment in Two Upper San Joaquin Valley Reservoirs,* while a corresponding thesis might be *An Experience-Based Model for Maximizing Water Containment in Two West Coast States.*

Projects are context-specific, while the generalizability inherent in theses affords widespread applicability. In the examples above, both projects are demographically and thus geographically limited, while theses and dissertations offer the important advantage of generalizability or widespread applicability to many other contexts. Thus, in the example above the project related to Bilingual Hispanic aides might be based on the policies, procedures, salaries and other considerations in specific school districts----while the thesis related to Bilingual Hispanic aides might be usable in Florida, Texas, or New York school districts or in other districts employing significant numbers of Bilingual Hispanic aides.

The fictitious titles below are a representative group of projects that should give you a clear idea as to the scope and intention of projects:

A Handbook for Science Camp Operation in Harris County Schools

An Alameda County Resource Directory of Services for A.D.D Patients

A Procedural Manual for Emergency Response to Medical AirEvacuation Activities in Langston County

Board-Approved Guidelines for Evaluating Development of Hospital Assistants

A Procedural Manual for Maintaining Operation of Hayward City Offices During Employee Job Actions

A Manual for Selecting, Hiring, Orientation and Placement of San Diego County Social Workers

What is common to all of these projects? The answer is that all focus on a *definite activity* within a *specific agency,* thus limiting the usefulness of each outcome beyond its original context. One or more attempts to use the *Manual for*

Selecting, Hiring, Orientation and Placement of San Diego County Social Workers in another county might result in undesirable outcomes. Why? That manual might not fit another context because its selection criteria, hiring practices, timelines, bargaining agreements and other requirements and constraints were unique to that county.

The title of this chapter carries the notion that projects might be more workable alternatives for some persons. Who might these persons be?

The answer depends on two considerations. One is your work context and the second is your long-range career plans. Frequently, you can use a certain handbook, manual, procedure, curriculum guide, operations guide or other production on your job. You should use the project option, especially if you have no further plans about completing the doctorate. If you are interested in the doctorate, you should be aware that noted professors and scholars in some doctoral programs rely heavily on the nature and quality of your thesis when evaluating your application for entrance. This means that if you want to study with a certain noted scholar in a doctoral program, you should pursue a thesis.

> *The best ideas for projects come from practitioners. Talk to your public agency or business supervisor about problems. Frequently, discussions will reveal the need for projects that can solve those problems.*

Projects require adherence to the same scholarly standards as that required in development of theses.

You can understand the organization of *projects* by comparing it to that of theses (and dissertations). You will recall that one version of the *basic framework for theses or dissertations* , introduced in Chapter 4, is:

Chapter I - <u>Introduction and Background of the Study</u>
    Statement of the Problem
    Significance of the study
    Statement of the hypothesis(es)
    Operational Definitions
    Assumptions and Limitations
    Delimitations of the Study

Chapter II - <u>Review of the Related Literature</u>

Chapter III - <u>Methodology and Procedure</u>
    Setting of the Study
    Population and Sample
    Design of the Study
        Null Hypotheses (if appropriate)
        Criterion/Alpha levels
        Statistical Method
        Instrumentation
        Data collection procedures
        Data analysis

Chapter IV - <u>Analysis of Findings</u>

Chapter V - <u>Summary, Conclusions, Implications and Recommendations for Further Study</u>

Using the fictitious project title *A Handbook for Science Camp Operation in Harris County Schools,* it is easy to see the comparison to the four-chapter outline of a *project:*

Chapter I - <u>Introduction and Background of the Study</u>
    Rationale and Intended Application of the Project
    Statement of the Problem
    Significance of the project
    Operational Definitions)
    Assumptions and Limitations Related to the Project
    Delimitations of the Project

Chapter II - Review of the Related Literature
    Rationale for Science Camp in   Elementary Schools
    Basic Approaches to Science Camp Operation in America
    State Laws Governing Science Camp Operation
    Criteria for Effective Handbooks
    Summary

Chapter III - Methodology and Procedure
    Setting of the Study
    Identification of Salient Elements of Science Camp Programs
    Examination of Selected Existent Science Camp Programs
    Selection of Elements for Inclusion in this Handbook
    Pilot Testing of Handbook Procedures

Chapter IV - Analysis of Findings
    Presentation of Findings
    The Completed Handbook

Generally, projects use a four-chapter format, with the actual project presented in Chapter 4, following the presentation of associated findings surfaced during the investigation.

Occasionally, your five-chapter thesis might result in a product. This happens when the central interest of a thesis is generation of an explicit model. Many chairpersons and faculty members will insist on inclusion (in Chapter 4) of the actual product of such developmental procedures as *validation* of the effectiveness of those procedures. Such validation would, of course, necessitate extensive pilot testing. An example of this situation is a (fictitious) thesis entitled, *A Procedure for Modifying Curricular Content to Include Hispanic-American Historical and Cultural Interests.* In this thesis, you would have to include the model procedure, timelines, persons involved, and other procedural aspects.

Under such circumstances, the resulting thesis will adhere, more or less, to the *basic framework for theses or dissertations*, introduced in Chapter 4 and shown in the *first* example above. The only modification necessary is insertion of the project at the end of Chapter 4, immediately after reporting the findings.

A look at the three types of projects: *Research, Design, and Professional Portfolio.* The three project patterns, *research, design* and *professional portfolio* projects, share one important quality in common: each must be designed for and "fit" specific applications. By contrast, theses have generalizability and reasonably widespread applicability as their strong points. However, these projects have one major point in common with theses. They must adhere to the same scholarly standards.

Research Projects. *Research* projects typically result in informational or procedural handbooks, policy or teaching activity manuals, curricular guides or operational frameworks. An example of such a project could be *A Handbook for Teaching Gifted Hispanic 3rd Graders*, or *A Manual for the Recruitment, Training and Placement of Bilingual Hmong Aides.* Occasionally, research projects lead to new solutions to problems, accompanied by the design and use of new technologies or materials.

A *Research* project requires the same first three chapters as a thesis: Problem, Review of the Literature, and Methodology. The first three chapters should accomplish the following:

1. Make a scholarly case for the research project, based on findings in the literature and your research-based knowledge of field needs. You can make the strongest case when you can show that your school district, city offices, utility

company or other agency has expressed a need for the project, in writing.

2. Thoroughly review most if not all existent similar projects, in the interest of deriving the best wisdom from them, a synthesis to be applied to the current project.

3. Clearly detail all steps and procedures to be followed from the beginning to the end in development of the research project.

In most instances, five major sections comprise the Research project:

1. Chapter I: The Problem
2. Chapter II: Review of the Related Literature
3. Chapter III: Method and Procedure
4. Chapter IV: The Project and Related Findings
5. Chapter V: Critique of the Project

Let's look at a representative section that might be part of the (fictitious) project mentioned above, *A Handbook for Teaching Gifted Hispanic 3rd Graders.*   It is important to note that the language as well as the general organization is identical to that of any well-crafted thesis.

Chapter 1

THE PROBLEM

Recent legislation in California provided for a Gifted and Talented (G.A.T.E) program that replaced the Mentally Gifted Minors (M.G.M) program. Consistent with provisions of the permissive Educational Code in the state, the G.A.T.E. program gives school districts the option of applying for operating funds without being required to do so (_____1981).

Irrespective of choices made by school districts, the literature shows that most school districts continue to fail at identification and meaningful differentiation of gifted children. The problem is compounded in the instance of Hispanic children; that is, in spite of certain well-known problems related to second language acquisition, many Hispanic children are, in fact, gifted and talented, and should be identified and given the full capabilities of the state legislation.

Statement of the Problem

Unfortunately, the great majority of gifted children are likely to spend most of their time in regular classrooms because of lack of funds for specialists and related services (_____1980, 3-9). The problem is likely to be compound for Hispanic children because of problems related to identification.

It is important for teachers of gifted Hispanic children, and other children as well, to understand their special needs and to provide instruction for purposes of development of their higher mental processes within regular classes. Thus, the problem researched in the present study was that of development and presentation of an expedient method for identifying, differentiating, and providing appropriate instruction for gifted and talented Hispanic children.

Statement of the Project

The central interest of this project was development of a handbook for use by teachers of Hispanic children...

The major features important for incorporation into the handbook were:

1. Ease of use for informal assessment in the process of identifying gifted and talented Hispanic students;

2. Usability by all regular classroom teachers;

3. A comprehensive set of techniques for...

The following are a few representative (albeit fictitious) examples of M.A. *research* projects:

A Statewide Resource Directory of Comprehensive Services for Child Amputees.

Callison County Curriculum Content Standards Handbook, Grade 5.

An Operational Guide for the Hiring and Use of Consultants in River City Offices.

A Central Reference Curricular Framework for Use of Six Different Basal Readers, K-6.

A Procedural Manual for Initial Intake of HIV Diagnosed Patients.

Design Projects. This type of project involves both design and production of immediately usable outcomes that are currently relevant and timely in the context of a defined sphere of work. You should base the design on findings in relevant research literature of your field. Design projects typically result in instructional and other applications in the real world. Computerized video programs, new applications for the Internet, and new set designs for stage productions are good examples.

Of greatest importance is evidence of student thoroughness in working through all aspects of design and development, from the initial identification of need through defense. You should use scholarly language in the related research. However, the actual project use the language and jargon of ultimate users. For example, a film project should be consistent in all respects with similar projects in the related real-world field.

Apart from the actual applications, the processes of scholarly development and presentation of design projects are identical to those of research projects. The same is true of the format for scholarly presentation.

A few examples of design projects, all fictitious, are:

A New Low-Budget Television Game Show for Persons of All Ages

A User-Friendly Approach for DOS - MacIntosh Crosstalk

An Electric Car Design that Reduces Energy Requirements by Seven Percent

A Model Web-Page for Internet Direct-Sale Authors and Writers

Beyond Geoboards: An Economical, Teacher-Friendly Kindergarten Math Approach

Professional Portfolio Projects. In some fields, colleges and universities now require the professional portfolio as a terminal scholarly research option. This is true of fields like communications, advertising, and some business areas. Professional portfolios are documents that incorporate both research production procedures and a finished product aimed at demonstrating competence in a given field. Apart from the learning experiences involved, they are extremely helpful in "selling" graduates to prospective employers.

The scholarly research and presentation approach for professional portfolios adhere basically to the same format introduced earlier. The only difference is that you must present the portfolio project separately from the formal scholarly document. Examples of portfolio projects are dramatic productions, advertising layouts or campaigns, television program pilots and similar products.

Summary

The major difference between *projects* and *theses* is extent of generalizability. Projects usually are limited in usability to specific areas, communities, school districts, hospitals and other organizations with similar demographic conditions.

Typically, projects are context-specific manuals, guidelines, directories and other *products* immediately useful and applicable to certain agencies. By contrast, theses usually focus on *generalizable* findings usable in most if not all organizations of similar demography engaged in a given activity.

There are three project patterns, *research, design* and *professional portfolio* projects. They share one important quality in common: each must be designed for and "fit" specific applications.

**TIP BOX 5: A CALENDAR FOR DEVELOPMENT
OF YOUR PROJECT**

You must design your project for immediate use in your chosen field. This means that it must be compatible with the conventions, terminology, legalities and past practices of that field. A letter of need from an external agency will "sell" your faculty committee on a project. You should begin to develop ideas and topics for your project while taking required coursework, no later than the first day you enroll in *Research Methods.* Before you are eligible for formal faculty advisement, you can develop original topics. Follow the sequence below and you will avoid many problems along the way.

1. Keep a file of all term papers and lecture notes of all of your courses taken. This material will help (a) when you formulate your faculty advisory committee and (b) during required oral examinations.

2. Unless instructed otherwise, write all term papers in the style manual format required by your department.

3. Look for possible *project* topics in your interest area in *Master's Abstracts* and *Dissertation Abstracts,* two sources present in all college and university libraries. Read *Recommendations for Further Research* and *Implications for Practice,* (in Chapter 5) in theses, dissertations and other projects. Develop a file of recommendations you find in completed studies and group them by content area and date.

5. Write as many titles as you can think of that "capture" your interest. Try to narrow your choices to *three* feasible projects, those that (a) are regularly accessible, (b) require reasonable resources, and (c) can be completed within the time you have allocated for completion of your Master's degree.

6. *Rule out the possibility of duplicating existent research* by asking your university reference librarian for a synonym-based computer search of a data bank of your field.

TIP BOX 5 (Continued)

7. On the basis of your interest, choose three of the five titles, and write a *two-page* proposal on each. *Be sure to include a statement about the computerized data search, including the date.*

8. Ask your *Research Methods* instructor for a critique of each proposal, then choose two of the three titles based on your interests and the reaction of your instructor.

7. While you wait for your instructor's critique, make appointments with supervisors of agencies that might be interested in each of the projects. Give the supervisor a copy of your proposal. Be prepared to (a) explain your proposed project in language used by the agency, and (b) ask for a letter of interest from the supervisor. *It is a good idea to talk to at least two separate agencies related to two separate projects.*

10. Develop the two proposals for submission to your committee. For each proposal, be sure to include (a) a letter of interest from an agency, and (b) a complete bibliography.

11. Take the two proposals to a faculty member (a) in whose classes you have done well and (b) interested in your content area. If possible, choose a senior, Full Professor----for reasons explained throughout this book.

12. If you receive a positive written reaction from the faculty member of your choice, schedule an appointment soon thereafter. During the appointment, ask that faculty member to serve as chairperson of your project committee.

9

A FEW PRACTICAL MATTERS AND WRAP-UP

Although the content of much of this chapter might seem redundant, several important aspects are in the realm of common sense. While they may seem excessive to those of you who have already considered them, they are nevertheless offered separately here because of their importance.

Whether you're a full-time student or a busy professional studying during your free time, you *must* work on it *daily*, without fail---even if your schedule permits only 30 minutes of work.

Rapid production and completion of terminal scholarly work require *continuity,* with no lapses. This point is extremely important to those of you who work a full-time job, and can only work on terminal scholarly activities after work hours.

When you experience lapses of no productivity in your research or actual writing, you threaten successful completion of your thesis, dissertation or project, for several reasons. The first and perhaps most important is that when you resume your work, you have to devote much if not most of the time available for that work session to review and update. In other words, you have to answer the question, "Where was I?" Frequently, you will need one or more work sessions in order to gain the necessary update!

Subtler perhaps, and quite variable among persons, is the possibility that you might lose confidence in the overall merits of your subject or study. Long time lapses away from your work often induce doubts about its overall merit.

The advocacy of an eager chairperson is central to the third reason you need regular work on your study. In addition to staying in touch frequently, prompt submission of new portions of your research is one of the best ways to maintain the eager support of your chairperson.

By now one or more of you might question the value of a mere 30 minutes of work as suggested in the caption above. The basic point is that the reading and review activity in that 30 minutes helps your mental continuity until you are able to do more work per session.

Careful attention to details related to documentation and other conventions in style manuals required by graduate departments will enhance the acceptance of your thesis, dissertation or project by committee members. This applies equally well to the organization and placement of front and end matter.

Let's start this section with the reminder that faculty members are individuals, with individual strengths, weaknesses, personal convictions, biases and different attitudes toward terminal scholarly activities of students. Here, we need to extend that point.

Committee members and chairpersons display markedly different attitudes toward student work. Some focus on the substantive aspects of theses, dissertations and projects. Others turn their attention to details related to documentation and conventions, especially those required by departments. It is not unusual to find certain committee members whose only comments or bases for opposition center on seemingly trivial things, like the organization of the captions on the title page, spacing of the table of contents page, or the language and tone of permission letters in the appendix!

When you carefully attend to details related to documentation and other conventions in style manuals required by your department, you tend to "de-fang" opposition by such faculty and committee members. You should give the same meticulous attention to organization and placement of front matter (title page, table of contents, table of figures) and end matter (appendixes, illustrations and bibliography).

Why should the progress of your work be disrupted or opposed by one or more committee members strictly on the basis of violated conventions? Why not remove that layer of opposition?

You should be able to use unobtrustive measures for seeking and analyzing data.

Many researchers tend to rely heavily on one or two sources of data and overlook one additional important source. That source is what one great book called *unobtrusive measures* (Webb, Campbell, Schwartz and Sechrest 1966).

As the name suggests, unobtrusive measures are those taken without involving or disturbing participants or respondents in studies. These measures, categorized as physical traces, archival data, and observations, are subtle: library withdrawals indicate increased interest in reading; the extent to which students cluster with others of their own backgrounds can indicate their intercultural attitudes; and posters, artifacts and other creations of their students can indicate some aspects of teacher effectiveness. You should never overlook these measures, because they can act as cross-validators of data taken through other measures.

These unobtrusive measures are all around us. Interested students should read:

Webb, E.J., Campbell, D.T., Schwartz, R.D., and Sechrest, L. 1966. *Unobtrusive Measures: Nonreactive Research in the Social Sciences.* **Chicago: Rand McNally College Publishing.**

If you need permission from various agencies for access to research data, remember to emphasize anonymity, confidentiality, and acceptable research ethics in your written requests for access.

Virtually all researchers need access to appropriate research contexts. For example, a researcher interested in the relationship between the quality of foster homes and the school performance of foster children needs access to school cumulative record folders. The same is true of a hospital researcher interested in the information-seeking behavior of, say, Hispanic mothers in well-baby clinics.

The proper and surest way to gain access to organized records related to research interests is through a direct request to appropriate persons in the agencies holding those records. Anonymity, confidentiality and acceptable research ethics are concerns of agencies reviewing requests for research. Some agencies also want to know the results of the research!

You should make a point of learning the name, title and address of the person who makes the final decision about research access. Following that, send a letter requesting research access to that person, emphasizing:

1. The strict uses to be made of the information.
2. A guarantee of confidentiality about the results.
3. A guarantee of anonymity of respondents and subjects.
4. A guarantee that research ethics will not be violated.
5. A clear statement of the specific dates and times that access will be needed.
6. A promise to make all research results available to that agency on request.

Whenever possible, you should attempt to use or modify *existent* questionnaires, opinionnaires or tests prior to developing your own.

The moral of this section is, simply, "don't re-invent the wheel." Like many other aspects throughout this book, this is an appeal to common sense.

For much non-experimental research, students must use surveys, opinionnaires, questionnaires, and even certain tests. Effective design of each one of these information-gathering vehicles requires considerable sophistication, frequently well beyond that possessed by the average graduate student. Also, a competent thesis, dissertation or project committee is likely to make a student present a thorough, scholarly defense of an information-gathering instrument devised (from the ground up) by that student.

Why not minimize obstacles? Why not find a survey, opinionnaire, questionnaire or test similar to what you need and modify it as little as possible? For example, a student interested in the opinions of Portuguese bilingual parents should attempt to find an existent instrument aimed at similar interests and simply modify it to fit specific content interest. Not only is such an instrument likely to be much easier to defend; there is a strong probability that you will enhance both its reliability and validity!

What are some sources of such existent instruments? Perhaps the best two sources are (1) theses, dissertations or projects written on similar or related topics; and (2) several published volumes on existent tests.   You can locate all of them with the help of a reference librarian.

Oral examinations related to terminal scholarly activities represent a long-standing tradition in graduate study. Both the focus and context of oral examinations vary widely among colleges and universities.

Many universities require oral examinations of Master's and doctoral candidates *after* final approval of their theses, dissertations or projects. The oral examination requirement stems from higher education tradition, from an era when oral examinations were primary avenues for assessing the capabilities of candidates for graduation.

While the tradition survives in most institutions, it has diminished in importance in most, primarily because of one major legal reason. One of the cornerstones of English common law is the principle of *estoppel*, which forbids a change after an individual has been led to rely on a belief. In other words, the college or university would find it difficult to defend the disqualification of a student after that student had successfully met all of the coursework and terminal scholarly writing requirements!

Still, "failure" in the oral examination can delay graduation. This means that you should prepare for them as thoroughly and effectively as possible.

How? First of all, you should be thoroughly familiar with the subject matter of your thesis, dissertation or project, with particular attention to (1) positions of authorities on the subject; (2) rival hypotheses to the ones made in your study; and (3) research methodology used in your study, quantitative and qualitative.

Second, you should remember the point made in Chapter 5, about the importance of retaining and reviewing the old class notes of professors on your M.A., doctoral or project committee. Awareness of the differential professional opinions, biases and attitudes of various committee members will help to remove considerable opposition during the oral examination.

Summary

It is extremely important to schedule *daily* work on your terminal scholarly document. Lapses of no productivity in research or actual writing are very threatening to successful completion of your thesis, dissertation or project. Daily work sessions, even short ones of 30 minutes, maintain continuity and avoid constant review and update, loss of confidence in your study, and loss of the advocacy of your chairperson.

While many committee members and chairpersons focus on the substance of theses, dissertations and projects, others turn their attention to documentation and other convention details. It is not unusual to find certain committee members whose only comments or bases for opposition focus on seemingly trivial mechanical aspects. When you attend to such details in style manuals required by your department, the effect is one of "de-fanging" opposition by certain faculty and committee members.

Unobtrusive measures are those taken without disturbing participants or respondents involved in studies. These measures should never be overlooked, as they frequently function as cross-validators of data taken through other measures.

Whenever possible, you should attempt to use or modify *existent* questionnaires, opinionnaires or tests prior to developing your own. The best two sources of these existent instruments are (1) theses, dissertations or projects written on similar or related topics; and (2) several published volumes on existent tests, all of which can be located by a reference librarian.

If you face the requirement of an oral examination following completion of your terminal scholarly activity, you prepare for it as thoroughly and effectively as possible. Effective preparation is possible through attention to: (1) the subject matter of your thesis, dissertation or project, with particular attention to (a) positions of authorities on the subject; (b) rival hypotheses to the ones made in your study; and (c) research methodology used in your study, quantitative and qualitative. You should also review the old class notes of professors on your M.A., doctoral or project committee. Your awareness of the differential professional opinions, biases and attitudes of various committee members will help to remove considerable opposition during your oral examination.

BIBLIOGRAPHY

American Educational Research Association. 1986. *Handbook of Research on Teaching.* Edited by M.C. Wittrock. New York: Macmillan.

American Institute of Physics. 1978. *Style Manual for Guidance in the Preparation of Papers.* 3d. Ed. New York: American Institute of Physics.

American Psychological Association. 1994. *Publication Manual of the American Psychological Association.* 3rd Ed. Washington, D.C.: American Psychological Association.

Anastasi, A. 1968. *Psychological Testing.* New York: Macmillan.

Aronson, J. 1994. "A Pragmatic View of Thematic Analysis." *The Qualitative Report, 2* (1).

Berdie, D.R., and Anderson, J.F. 1974. *Questionnaires: Design and Use.* Metuchen, N.J.: Scarecrow Press.

Borg, W.R., and Gall, M.D. 1983. *Educational Research: An Introduction.* New York: Longman.

Buttram, J. 1987. "Effective Teaching Practices." *Educational Leadership*, April.

Campbell, W.G., and Ballou, S.V. 1990. *Form and Style: Theses, Reports, Term Papers*, 8th Ed. Boston: Houghton-Mifflin.

Campbell, D.T., and Stanley, J.C. 1966. *Experimental and Quasi-Experimental Designs for Research.* Chicago: Rand McNally and Company.

Council of Biology Editors, Committee on Form and Style. 1983. *CBE Syyle Manual.* 5th Ed. Washington, D.C: American Institute of Biological Sciences.
Cozby, P.C., Worden, P.E., and Kee, D.W. 1989.*Research Methods in Human Development.* Mountain View, CA: Mayfield Publishing.

Crowl, T.K. 1996. *Fundamentals of Educational Research.* 2D Ed. Madison, WI: Brown and Benchmark.

Denzin, N.K. 1983. "Interpretive Interactionism." In G. Morgan, ed., *Beyond Method: Strategies for Social Research.* 129-46. Beverly Hills: Sage Publications.

Dillman, D.A. 1995. *Mail and Telephone Surveys: The Total Design Method.* New York: Wiley-Interscience.

Drew, C.J., Hardman, M.L., and Hart, A.W. 1996. *Designing and Conducting Research: Inquiry in Education and Social Science.* Boston: Allyn and Bacon.

Dunkin, M.J., and Biddle, B.J. 1974. *The Study of Teaching.* New York: Holt, Rinehart and Winston.

Eichelberger, R.T. 1989. *Disciplined Inquiry: Understanding and Doing Educational Research.* New York: Longman.

Eisner, E. 1979. *The Educational Imagination.* New York: Macmillan.

Eisner, Eliot W. 1991. *The Enlightened Eye: Qualitative Inquiry and the Enhancement of Educational Practice* New York: Macmillan Publishers.

Eisner, E.W., and Peshkin, A. 1990. "Introduction." In *Qualitative Inquiry in Education: The Continuing Debate* , eds. E.W. Eisner and A. Peshkin. New York: Teachers College Press.

Fowler, F.J. 1993. *Survey Research Methods.* Applied Social Research Methods Series, Vol. 1. Newbury Park, CA: Sage Publications.

Gable, G. 1994. "Integrating Case Study and Survey Research Methods: An Example in Information Systems." *European Journal of Information Systems.* 3(2): 112-26.

Gage, N.L. 1972. *Teacher Effectiveness and Teacher Education.* Palo Alto: Pacific Books.

Gage, N.L. 1978. *The Scientific Basis of the Art of Teaching.* New York: Teachers College Press.

Geertz, C. 1973. *The Interpretation of Cultures.* New York: Basic Books.

Ghiselli, E. E. 1964. *Theory of Psychological Measurement.* New York: McGraw-Hill.

Good, Carter V. 1963. *Introduction to Educational Research.* 2d. Ed. New York: Appleton-Century-Crofts.

Guilford, J.P. 1967. *The Nature of Human Intelligence.* New York: McGraw-Hill.

Hagberg, H.M. 1983. *Don't Be Teachin' Jovita Wrong: An Exploration of Reading Instruction in Four Urban Third Grade Classrooms.* Ph.D diss., Stanford University, Palo Alto, CA.

Hittleman, D.R., and Simon, A. 1997. *Interpreting Educational Research: An Introduction for Consumers of Research.* Columbus, Ohio: Merrill.

Isaac, S., and Michael, W.B. 1989. *Handbook in Research and Evaluation.* 2d Ed. San Diego: EDITS Publishers.

Kaplan, A. 1964. *The Conduct of Inquiry: Methodology for Behavioral Science.* San Francisco: Chandler Publishing.

Kaplan, B., and Duchon, D. 1988. "Combining Qualitative and Quantitative Methods in Information Systems Research: A Case Study." *MIS Quarterly,* 12(4): 571-86.

Keppel, G. 1973. *Design and Analysis: A Researcher's Handbook.* Englewood Cliffs, NJ: Prentice-Hall.

Kerlinger, F.N. 1973. *Foundations of Behavioral Research. 2nd. Ed.* New York: Holt, Rinehart and Winston.

Lapin, L.L. 1987. *Statistics for Modern Business Decisions.* New York: Harcourt Brace Jovanovich.

Lee, A. 1991. "Integrating Positivist and Interpretive Approaches to Organizational Research." *Organization Science,* 2(4): 342-65.

Lieberson, S. 1985. *Making it Count: The Improvement of Social Research and Theory.* Berkeley: University of California.

Lincoln, Y., and Guba, E. 1985. *Naturalistic Inquiry.* Beverly Hills, CA: Sage.

Lippitt, G. 1973. *Visualizing Change.* Arlington, VA: NTL Learning Resources.

Mason, E.J., and Bramble, W.J. 1997. *Research in Education and the Behavioral Sciences.* Madison, WI: Brown and Benchmark.

Mathison, S. 1988. "Why Triangulate?" *Educational Researcher.* 17(2): 13-17.

McMillan, J.H. 1996. *Educational Research: Fundamentals for the Consumer.* New York: HarperCollins Publishers.

McNemar, Q. 1962. *Psychological Statistics.* 3rd. Ed. New York: John Wiley.

Merriam, S. 1988. *Case Study Research in Education: A Qualitative Approach.* San Francisco: Jossey-Bass.

Mitchell, M., and Jolley, J. 1988. *Research Design Explained.* New York: Holt, Rinehart and Winston.

Orlich, D.C., Harder, R.J., Callahan, R.C., Kravas, C.H., Kauchak, D.P., Pendergrass, R.A., and Keogh, A. J. 1985. *Teaching Strategies: A Guide to Better Instruction. 2d. Ed.* Lexington, Mass: D.C. Heath.

Patton, M.Q. 1990. *Qualitative Evaluation and Research Methods.* Newbury Park, CA: Sage Publications.

Popham, W. J. 1967. *Educational Statistics: Use and Interpretation.* New York: Harper and Row.

Resta, P.E. and Baker, R.L. 1967. *Formulating the Research Problem.* Inglewood, California: Southwest Laboratory for Educational Research and Development.

Roscoe, John T. 1969. *Fundamental Research Statistics for Behavioral Sciences.* New York: Holt, Rinehart and Winston.

Robinson, G.E. 1985. "Effective Schools Research: A Guide to School Improvement." *Concerns in Education.* Arlington, VA: Educational Research Service.

Rossi, P.H., Wright, J.D., and Anderson, A.B. 1983. *Handbook of Survey Research.* San Diego: Academic Press.

Russell Sage Foundation. 1967. *Survey Research in the Social Sciences,* edited by C.Y. Glock. New York: Russell Sage Foundation.

Salant, P., and Dillman, D.A. 1994. *How to Conduct Your Own Survey.* New York: John Wiley.

Schuman, H., and Presser, S. 1981. *Questions and Answers in Attitude Surveys: Experiments on Question Form, Wording and Context.* New York: Academic Press.

Schumacher, S., and McMillan, J.H. 1993. *Research in Education: A Conceptual Introduction.* New York: HarperCollins *College* Publishers.

Sharp, Vicki F. 1979. *Statistics for the Social Sciences.* Boston: Little, Brown.

Slade, C. 1997. *Form and Style: Research Papers, Reports, Theses.* Boston: Houghton-Mifflin.

Smith, M.L., and Glass, G. V. 1987. *Research and Evaluation in Education and the Social Sciences.* Englewood Cliffs, N.J.: Prentice-Hall.

Soltis, J.F. 1990. "The Ethics of Qualitative Research." In E.W. Eisner, ed. *Qualitative Inquiry in Education,* 247-57. New York: Teachers College Press.

Stallings, J., and Kaskowitz, D. 1974. *Follow-Through Classroom Observation Evaluation, 1972-73.* (SRI Project URU-7370). Menlo Park: Stanford Research Institute.

Sternberg, D. 1981. *How to Complete and Survive a Doctoral Dissertation.* New York: St. Martin's Press.

Sudman, S., and Bradburn, N. 1982. *Asking Questions: A Practical Guide to Questionnaire Design.* San Francisco: Jossey-Bass.

Turabian, Kate L. 1973. *A Manual for Writers of Term Papers, Theses and Dissertations.* 4th Ed. Chicago: University of Chicago Press.

United States Department of Education. 1986. *What Works: Research About Teaching and Learning.* Washington, D.C.: United States Department of Education.

University of Chicago Press. 1993. *The Chicago Manual of Style.* 14th Ed. Chicago: University of Chicago Press.

Vierra, A., Pollock, J., and Golez, F. 1998. *Reading Educational Research. 3E Ed.* Columbus, Ohio: Merrill.

Vockell, E.L., and Asher, J.W. 1995. *Educational Research.* Second Edition. Columbus,Ohio: Prentice-Hall.

Warwick, D.P., and Lininger, C. 1975. *The Sample Survey: Theory and Practice.* New York: McGraw-Hill.

Webb, E.J., Campbell, D.T., Schwartz, R.D., and Sechrest, L. 1966. *Unobtrusive Measures: Nonreactive Research in the Social Sciences.* Chicago: Rand McNally College Publishing.

Webster, W. G. 1994. *Learner-Centered Principalship: The Principal as Teacher of Teachers.* Westport, CT: Praeger Publishers.

Wilson, S. 1979. "Explorations of the Usefulness of Case Study Evaluations." *Evaluation Quarterly*, *3*, 446-59.

SUBJECT INDEX